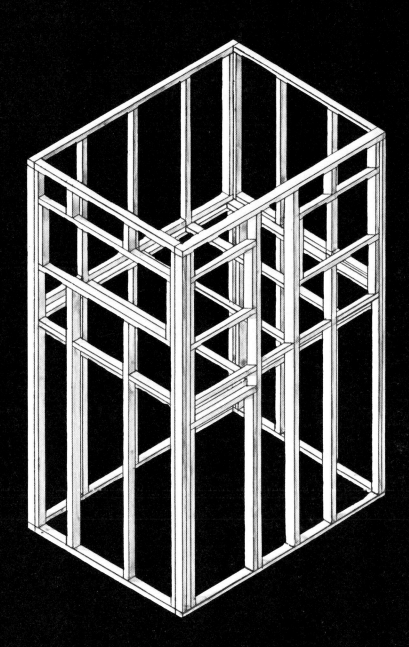

The Loft Book

The Loft Book

THIS BOOK IS DEDICATED TO
LEONARDO DAVINCI
CLAES OLDENBURG
MY MOM & POP

Jim Wilson

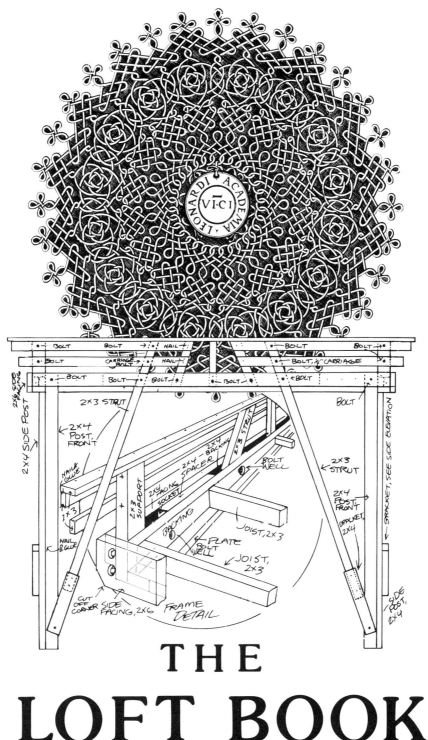

THE
LOFT BOOK

Running Press
Philadelphia, Pennsylvania

Printed in the United States of America

Distributed in Canada by Van Nostrand Reinhold Ltd., Ontario

Library of Congress Catalog Card Number 75-17047

ISBN 0-914 294-32-6 (Paperback Edition)
ISBN 0-914 294-33-4 (Library Edition)

Loft Book
Production Assistance by:
Elaine Brody
Sharon Green Pitts

Loft Book
Photography by:
Kas Schlots
Andrew Ralph
Jim Wilson

Written, Designed and Illustrated by
Jim Wilson

This book may be ordered directly from the publisher. Please include 25¢ postage.
Try your bookstore first.

Running Press, 38 South Nineteenth Street, Philadelphia, Pennsylvania 19103

PREMISE

The Loft Book is about the design, construction, furnishing and use of sleeping lofts.

You do not need to be an experienced designer or carpenter to use this book. The construction sections take the techniques of woodworking that apply to lofts, and present them in easy-to-understand visual form.

The design sections make the planning and execution of a loft much simpler for those who do not normally think in terms of design. Even experienced woodworkers will be helped greatly by these sections, as efficiency is the end result of good design. The planning kits are provided with grids and cutouts, so even drawing skills are unnecessary.

The information in this book is not confined only to lofts. It is concerned with the creative use of any limited space by the amateur. The same principles and methods apply to closets, bathrooms, hallways or home-built furniture.

Raftworks Tower, constructed by the author & Werner Krupp, 1973.
A sort of loft, on Cape Hatteras. All-Driftwood. First deck completed.

Table of Contents

8

ABOUT THE LOFT BOOK

Interior of **Starship Loft** designed and built by the author. Urethane foam wall covering. Queen size mattress. Photo by the author.

This book is the product of my ongoing love affair with lofts. My original interest in lofts grew out of necessity. In 1973 I was part of a design studio in Vermont. The idea was that two of us would live there in a giant studio, workshop, darkroom, and living space. The situation made a normal bedroom out of the question; so I built a loft.

The deck was four feet from the ceiling. If that seems like a low ceiling to you, remember that most bedroom activities take place in a prone or seated position. The expression "crawl into bed", isn't that far off the mark. And when you're sitting up, you're only about three feet tall. That first loft, though only 5 x 10 x 4, was roomy enough to seat six people very comfortably. Six people couldn't sleep in it, but it was terrific with three.

ABOUT THE LOFT BOOK

Lofts somehow seem to attract crowds. In this case it was the most comfortable room in the building. Music sounded better there, the light was softer and the view was better.

I painted one end of it flat black, and every other surface except the floor was covered by one-inch-thick foam. Affixed to the black wall were silver gummed stars, and a six-inch cutout photo of the Earth. The Earth was handcolored and mounted two inches away from the wall. I built a little projector high into the opposite wall. It beamed a round spot that exactly illuminated the earth cutout, and made it appear to float in space. The effect was that of a picture window in the side of a spacecraft. Combined with the foam wall covering for sound proofing, it was a very restful place.

When fellow designer Werner Krupp and I put together Winooski Raftworks, another studio-workshop-living space, we had to build lofts because of space problems. There we needed not only sleeping room, but storage space as well. Again the loft became my favorite spot.

I began to realize that lofts fulfill a psychological as well as physical need. Lofts are spaces you can create for yourself. With a loft you are not dependent on the original shape of your room. It's a place that can be exactly what you want, and you don't need to buy land to build it. You can start thinking of a room as a place to park your loft, a sort of indoor trailer park. A loft can contain your sleeping, storage, and entertainment areas. That means you can get by with a place containing only a kitchen, bathroom and work space. It's a great way to save money. In my case, that means I don't have to work as much to live.

Because this is the only book on lofts to date, I've tried to include all the basic information you'll need to build your own loft. Knowing that most people have never built anything on this scale, I've devoted two chapters on the building techniques utilized.

For space reasons, I've had to assume that you know how to use a ruler and cut wood with a saw. I have included nailing, though, as that's not so obvious. There's a very short chapter on electric wiring. I don't assume anything about electricity, therefore I've drawn a picture of the circuit. Even if you can't read, you'll be able to wire a loft.

Because lighting is such an important part of a loft, or anyplace for that matter, there is a chapter devoted to that subject. As part of the chapter there are plans for a special state-of-the-art lighting fixture I've designed for lofts.

The loft pictorial section is to acquaint you with some of the possibilities of loft design and decoration. Most of them are not by professional builders.

There are plans for eight lofts here. You can build one exactly to the plans, or mix features from different designs to suit your fancy or needs. The only tools needed are a saw, a drill, a knife, a wrench, and a good old hammer.

You'll need to do some planning of where to put the loft, and how big to make it. Since most people have trouble drawing things to scale, I've gone to a lot of hassle doing planning kits. By cutting things out of the book and moving them around on a grid, you can easily do a beautiful blueprint.

10

About cutting things out of a seven dollar book.

For one thing, if you take somebody to a movie it's going to cost at least $7.00 for two hours of entertainment. These planning kits will keep you occupied for days. There's nothing valuable on the back sides of the kit pages anyway. I recommend cutting the pieces out with an x-acto® knife, for a really neat job.

About the crass materialism of the deck grid cutout kit.

I'm really not saying you should have all that stuff in your loft. But if someone wants to put a refrigerator in their loft, who am I to stand in their way. Personally, I think it's decadent to have a refrigerator in a loft. My refrigerator is on the floor beside my loft; the exercise is good for me.

The Author's current loft: View of deck construction from below.

Author's Loft: Under construction. Four foot deck height.

Because music and acoustics are such important parts of loft living I have devoted a big chapter to audio. It'll help you have champagne music quality on a Ripple® budget.

If this book sells you on the idea of having a loft, but doesn't convince you that you can build one, there's a chapter on commercial loftbuilders that may help you trade someone money for a loft.

Building your own is best though, people will really be amazed when they see it. They'll probably want you to build them one, too. That's what happened to me, and is another reason why I wrote this book. All I have to do now is hand it to them and say, "You can build one for yourself."

About the design and illustration of **The Loft Book**.

I make a large percentage of my living designing other people's books. Normally I would be handed a one-piece manuscript. I would then select a type-face and specify the widths of columns and margins. After that I would either assign an illustrator the job, or illustrate it myself. Then the whole thing would be pasted up neatly and sent off to the printer's.

As it happened, I wrote this book in a lot of little sections. Since I was designing and illustrating it at the same time, that came about in small sections also. That's why the chapter on loft lighting doesn't bear much resemblance to the one on loft planning. I think they're better matched that way. The color illustrations are sketchy, because in most cases, that's exactly what they are; rough watercolor sketches. You won't have to worry about making your loft as nice as the picture that way. Anybody can build a loft slicker than my sketches. Reassuring, eh?

Behind some of the color illustrations, I'm sure you'll notice a pattern of blue lines. That's the grid I designed for the page layouts. Each page is pasted up on a grid sheet. The blue lines normally don't photograph when printed. However, in a few places throughout the book, I liked the way they looked and kept them as part of the composition.

12

Author's Loft: Foot of loft,
speaker and cassette rack on carpeted wall.

Chapter 1
Loft
Pictorial

Author's Loft: Mostly finished, with lighting unit & phone.

14

ATTIC LOFT

Dr. and Mrs. Leslie Bankoff are the owners of this unusual loft. The loft is actually the product of removal rather than building. Sections of the upper floor under the eaves were cut out, leaving the loft.

The result is far superior to the original space, a couple of stuffy attic rooms. The view from the floor below is really impressive. The stained glass, brass bed and plants give the loft a warmth needed to offset the huge expanse of the loft space.

Attic Loft: View of loft from floor below.

Photos by KAS

15

Attic Loft: View of loft from bed.

16

John Meade designed and built this loft for Chris Hebenstreit. Its construction is like that of a giant bed. The head and footboards are plywood, padded with foam and covered in wet-look vinyl. There are shelves on the sides, and a sliding door conceals a closet in the center.

Forest Loft

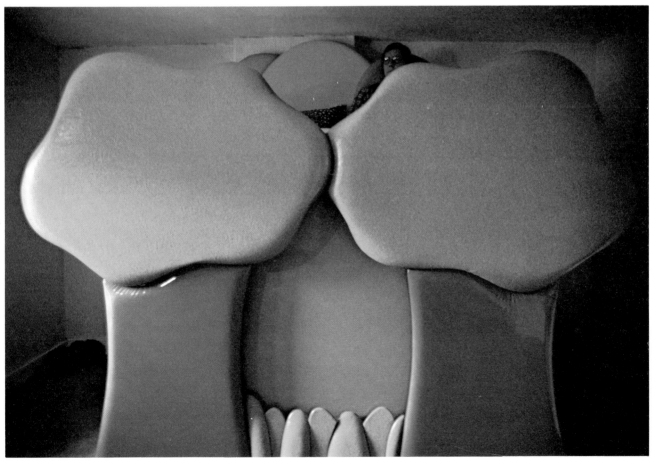

17

WERNER KRUPP'S LOFT

Werner Krupp's loft in Winooski Raftworks was cleverly worked into the back of a storefront showroom. It includes a desperately needed closet as part of the deck support.

The Winooski Raftworks is not in the raft business. Werner and I participated in a raft race down the Winooski River in Vermont. When we moved our studio to Philadelphia, we brought the raft along also. The raft makes a nice centerpiece for the room; and is a good place to pile things.

Winooski Raftworks: View of studio, Raft foreground, Loft rear.

Photos by KAS

18

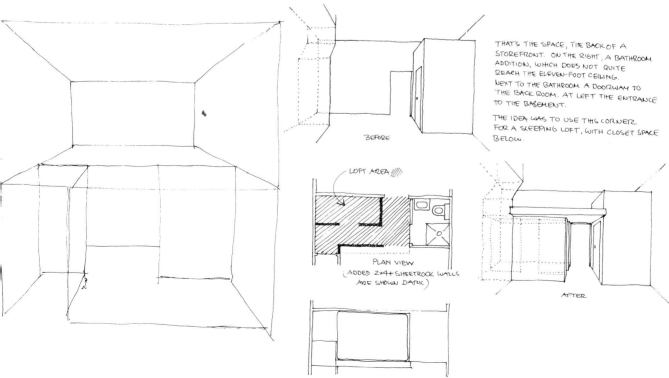

THAT'S THE SPACE, THE BACK OF A
STOREFRONT. ON THE RIGHT, A BATHROOM
ADDITION, WHICH DOES NOT QUITE
REACH THE ELEVEN-FOOT CEILING.
NEXT TO THE BATHROOM A DOORWAY TO
THE BACK ROOM. AT LEFT THE ENTRANCE
TO THE BASEMENT.

THE IDEA WAS TO USE THIS CORNER
FOR A SLEEPING LOFT, WITH CLOSET SPACE
BELOW.

BEFORE

LOFT AREA

PLAN VIEW
(ADDED 2×4+ SHEETROCK WALLS
ARE SHOWN DARK)

AFTER

19

Werner's sketches of his loft.

DOME LOFTS

Above: Darryl Digg's dome, Sharon, VT.
Below: David Timmon's dome, Plainfield, N.H.

A loft is the only way to make efficient use of the space inside a geodesic dome. Otherwise, you would end up with a very poor floor area to volume ratio. Andrew Ralph, noted dome authority (and a prince of a fellow) photographed these dome lofts in Vermont and New Hampshire.

20

PETER AND JOY
IN THEIR TINY LOFT

Peter is a writer and Joy is a sculptor. They live in a big, airy apartment over a porno bookshop. Peter built a table. Then he built this loft over a hallway. They have a full-size bedroom; the loft is only for special occasions. . .

ISAIAH & JULIA ZAGAR'S LOFT

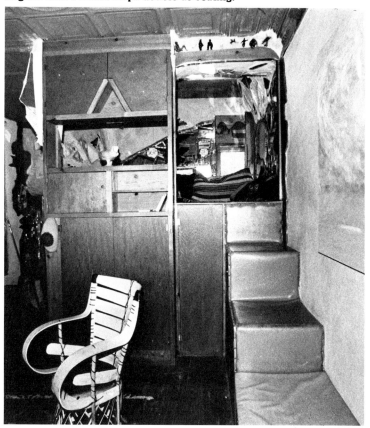

Isaiah and Julia are artists who travel all over Central and South America, bringing back Indian art for their gallery "Eyes" in Philadelphia. They have a beautiful house above the gallery, with an amazing loft. They built a big cabinet-closet; then cut out the ceiling above it. In the ceiling above that, there's a skylight. The inside walls are plaster, with mirrors, tiles and toys embedded.

Photos by KAS

Zagar's Loft: View from entry.

22

Zagar's Loft: View from upper level.

24

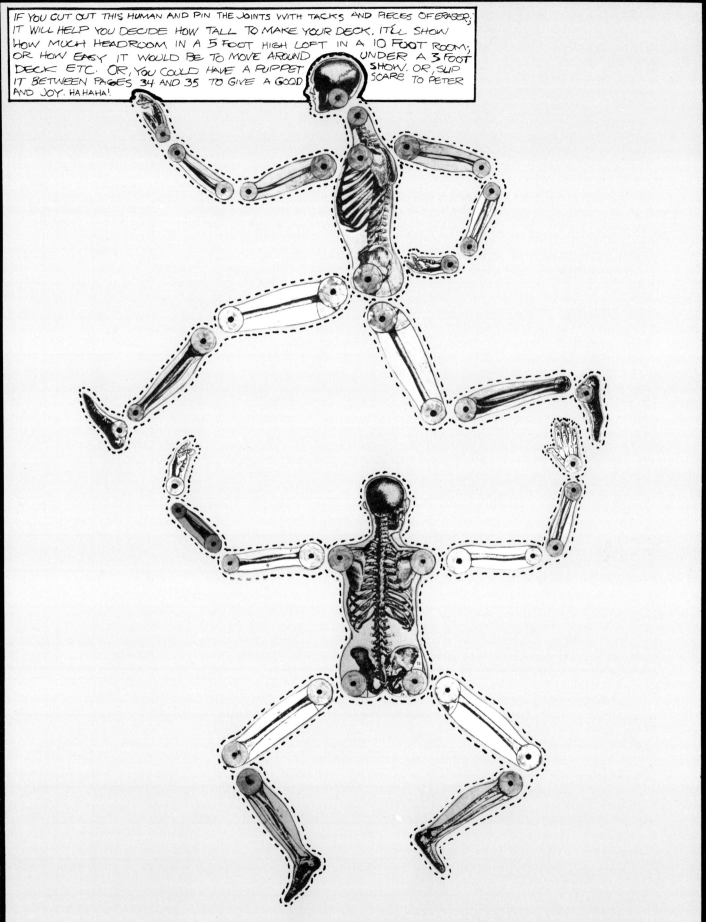

IF YOU CUT OUT THIS HUMAN AND PIN THE JOINTS WITH TACKS AND PIECES OF ERASER, IT WILL HELP YOU DECIDE HOW TALL TO MAKE YOUR DECK. IT'LL SHOW HOW MUCH HEADROOM IN A 5 FOOT HIGH LOFT IN A 10 FOOT ROOM; OR HOW EASY IT WOULD BE TO MOVE AROUND UNDER A 3 FOOT DECK ETC. OR, YOU COULD HAVE A PUPPET SHOW. OR, SLIP IT BETWEEN PAGES 34 AND 35 TO GIVE A GOOD SCARE TO PETER AND JOY. HAHAHA!

6 FT. ARTICULATED HUMAN, SCALE: 3/4" = 1'

Loft Planning
Kits Chapter 2

I have designed these kits to make your layout problems simpler. In order to plan your loft, it is essential to know how much space you are dealing with. In most cases there are factors such as windows, doors and protrusions. A door cannot normally be obstructed by a loft, so doors have to be taken into account in your initial planning.

The best way to avoid problems is to draw a plan of the room, indicating the shape of the room and its relation to the doors and windows.

The room planning grid and window and door cutouts will enable you to do an exact floor plan, to scale, of your room.

The deck layout grid serves the same function when you're planning the loft itself. In addition to a larger scale grid, I have included cutouts for most standard mattress sizes and some common appliances and accessories you may want in your loft.

Using Loft Room Grid

The first step is to transfer the floor plan of the room onto the grid. Each grid square is equivalent to a square foot of floor area. You will find a 10 or twenty foot tape measure very handy for this. What you will have after marking the outline of the room is a scale floor plan conveniently divided up into square feet. Then, using your tape measure, mark locations of windows and doors. After selecting door and window modules of the proper width, paste them in their correct locations. These will help you pick the best size loft, and facilitate locating the loft in the room.

Using Deck Layout Grid

This kit can be used in either of two ways. If space is limited and your deck size is restricted, you can use it to plan the most efficient layout of the deck. It will help you decide on a mattress size and let you see exactly how much space will be consumed by the furniture or accessories you're considering for your loft.

If room space is no problem you can use the grid to determine the size of the deck. Say you want a king size mattress, a TV, a stereo system, and a refrigerator in your loft: by laying the appropriate cutouts on the grid, you can easily see what size your deck will have to be to accomodate everything.

As you may have noticed, when the cutouts have been fitted into the grid in their final positions, the finished product makes a rather attractive collage. I would recommend cementing everything to the grid, and framing it for the wall of the loft. Your friends will be greatly impressed, and say things like ''I can't draw a straight line with a ruler myself.'' Then you will have the opportunity to say ''aw shucks, it was nothin'.''

10'

DECK LAYOUT GRID

SCALE: 3/4" = 1"
EACH GRID SQUARE EQUALS 1 SQUARE FOOT

27

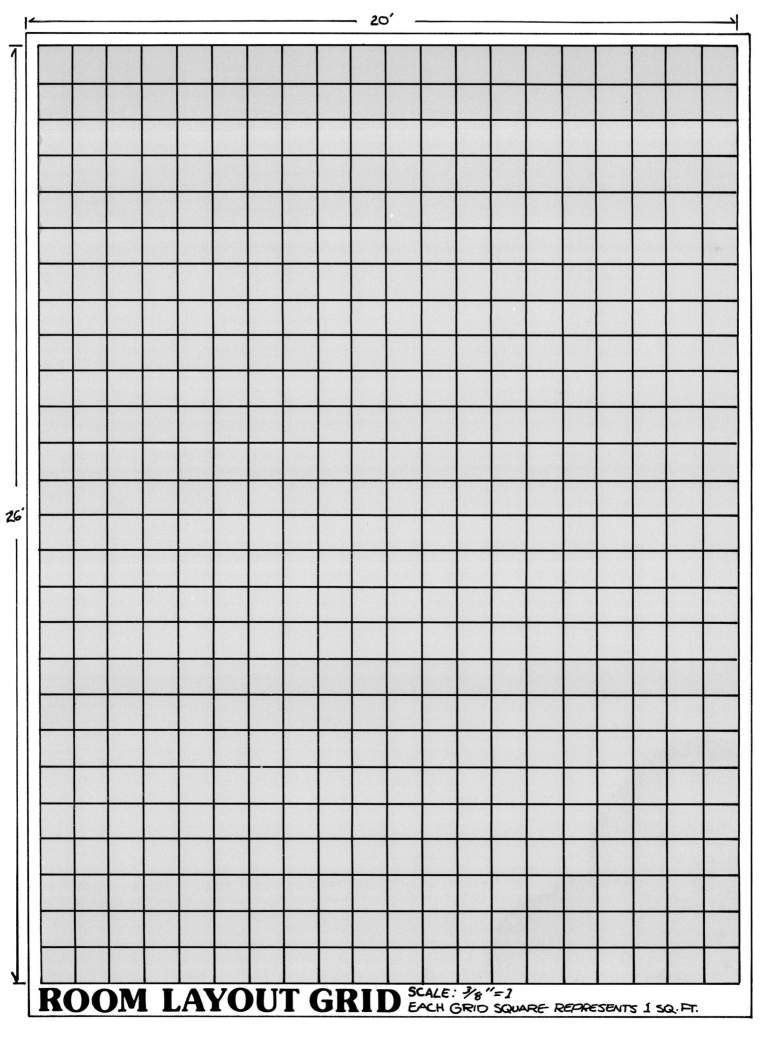

ROOM LAYOUT GRID SCALE: 3/8" = 1
EACH GRID SQUARE REPRESENTS 1 SQ. FT.

20'

26'

SCALE WINDOW & DOOR CUTOUTS

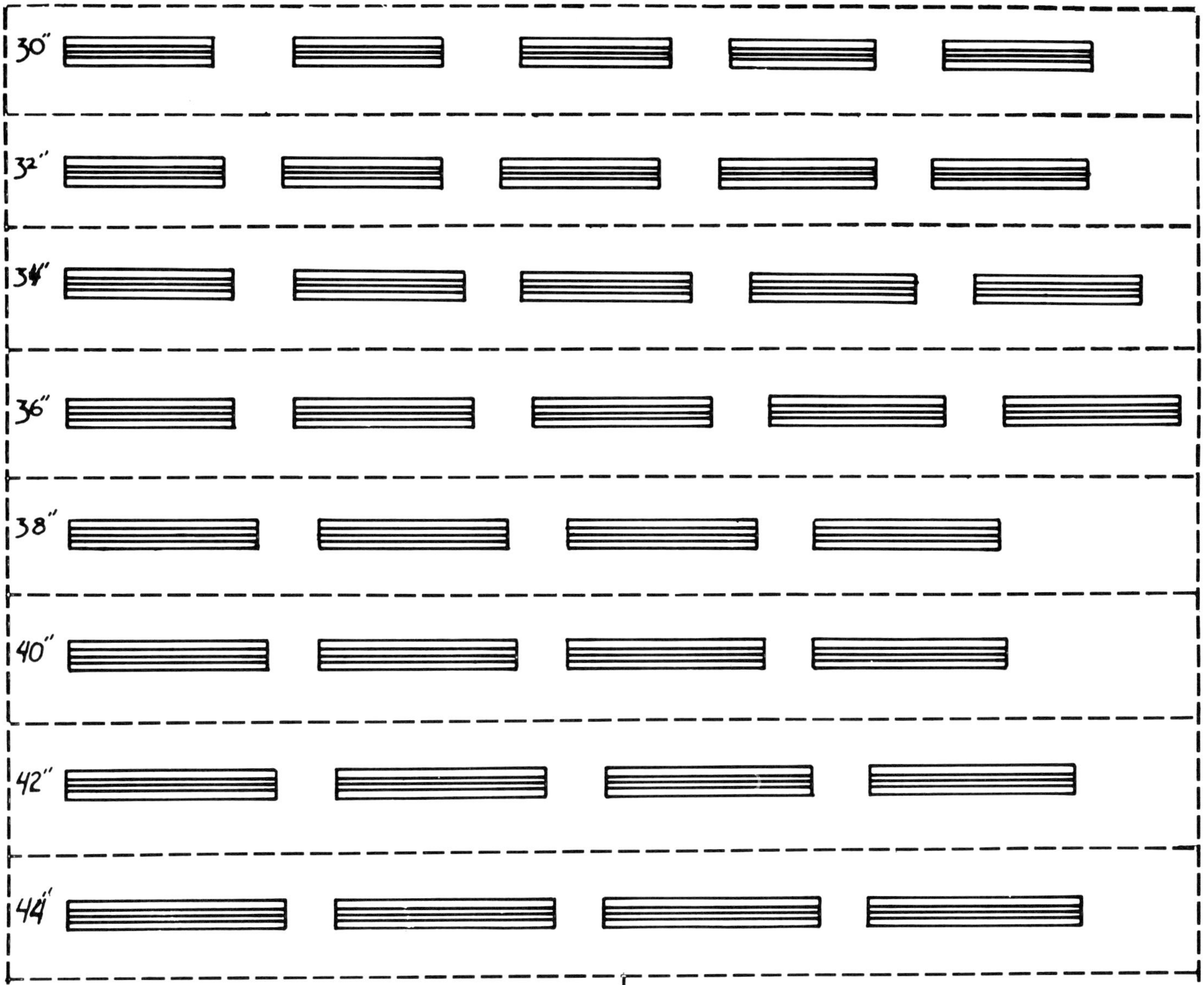

30"

32"

34"

36"

38"

40"

42"

44"

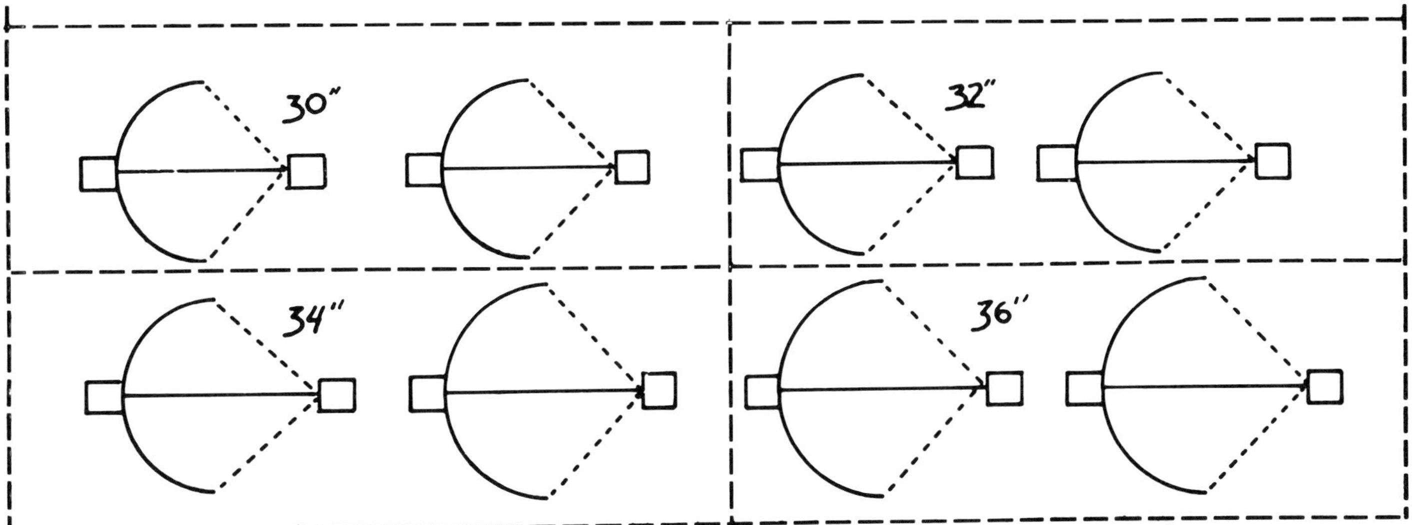

30"

32"

34"

36"

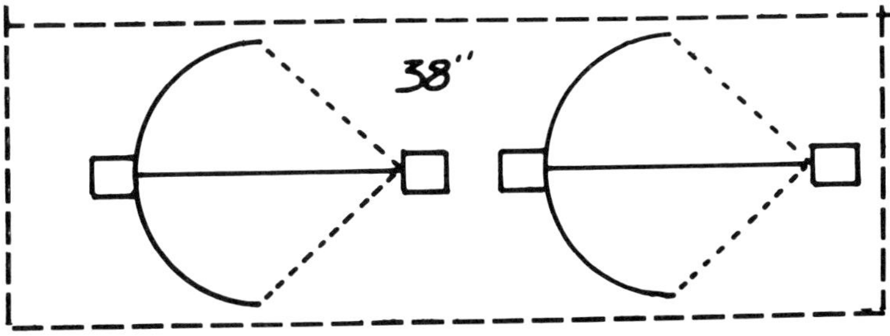

38"

How to use them:

After drawing room outline to scale on grid, measure windows & doors. Then, cut out proper size pieces. After taking position measurements, place windows & doors in scale position and affix them with glue or tape. If door opens inward, draw solid line over inside dotted door line. If outside, fill in outside one.

SCALE WINDOW & DOOR CUTOUTS

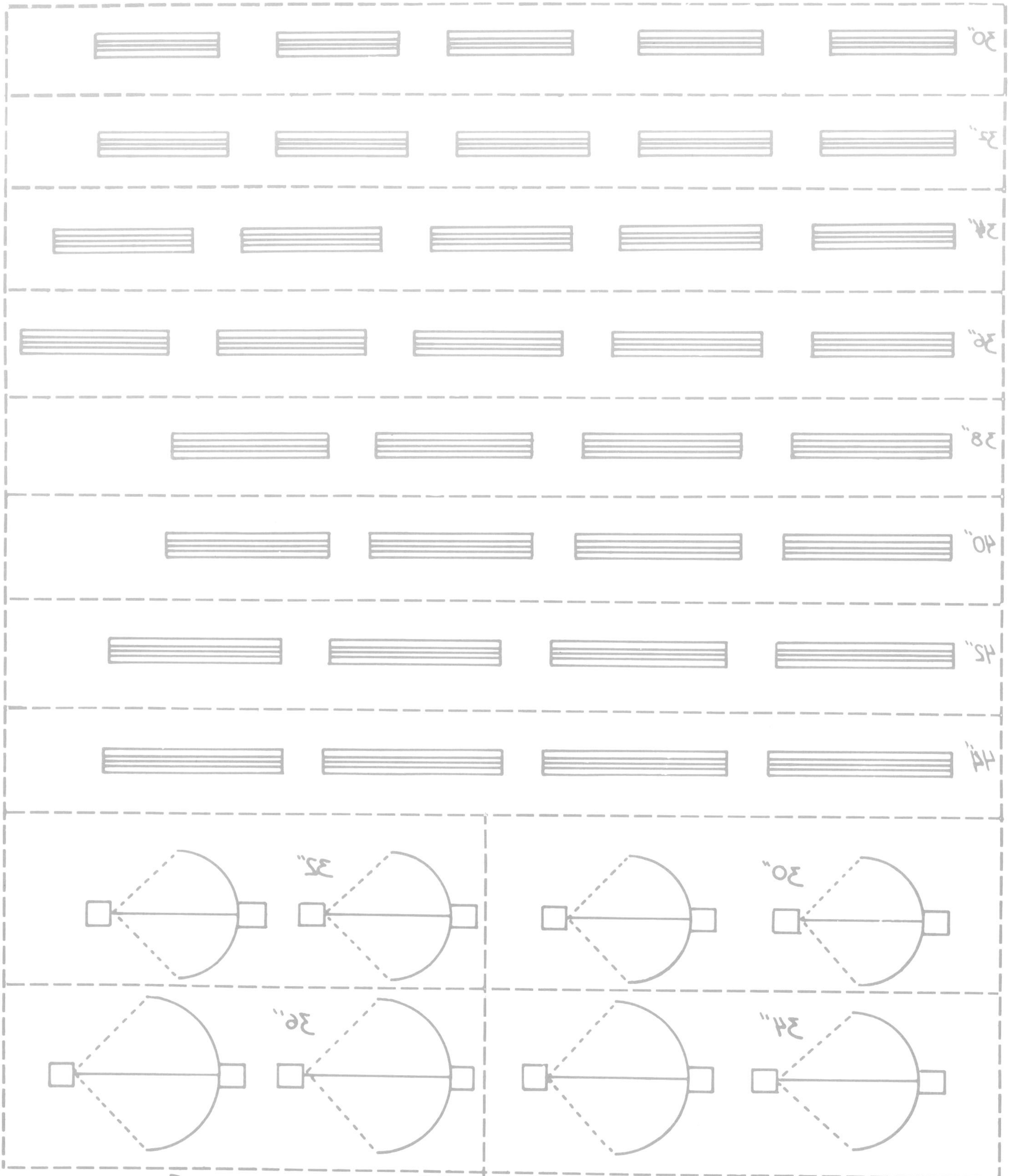

30" 32" 34" 36" 38" 40" 42" 44"

30" 32" 34" 36" 38"

How to use them:

After drawing room outline to scale on grid measure windows & doors. Then cut out proper size pieces. After taking position measurements, place windows & doors in scale position and affix them with glue or tape. If door opens inward, draw solid line over inside dotted door line. If outside, fill in outside one.

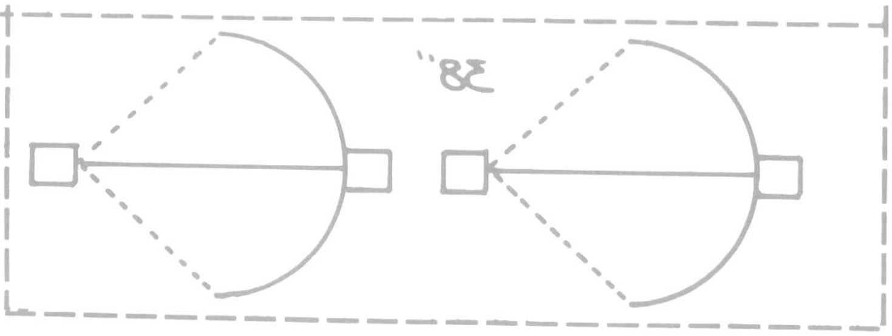

30

6'X10' DECK

SCALE: 3/8" = 1'

4'X8' DECK

8'X10' DECK

6'X8' DECK

10'X12' DECK

8'X12' DECK

Peter & Joy
On Queen Size Mattress

Three-Quarter Size Mattress

R.C.A. Portable Stereo

Dual® Changer

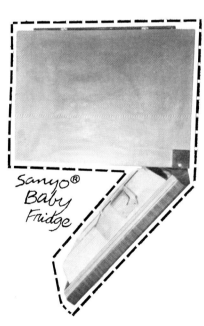

Sanyo®
Baby
Fridge

Plastic Milk
Crate
(Abbotts®)

upright
Sony® Tape Deck
laid flat

11 inch Portable TV
(Milonac®)

Princess™
Phone

D-500
TOUCHTONE™
Phone

Scale: ¾" = 1'

MATTRESS & FURNISHINGS CUTOUTS

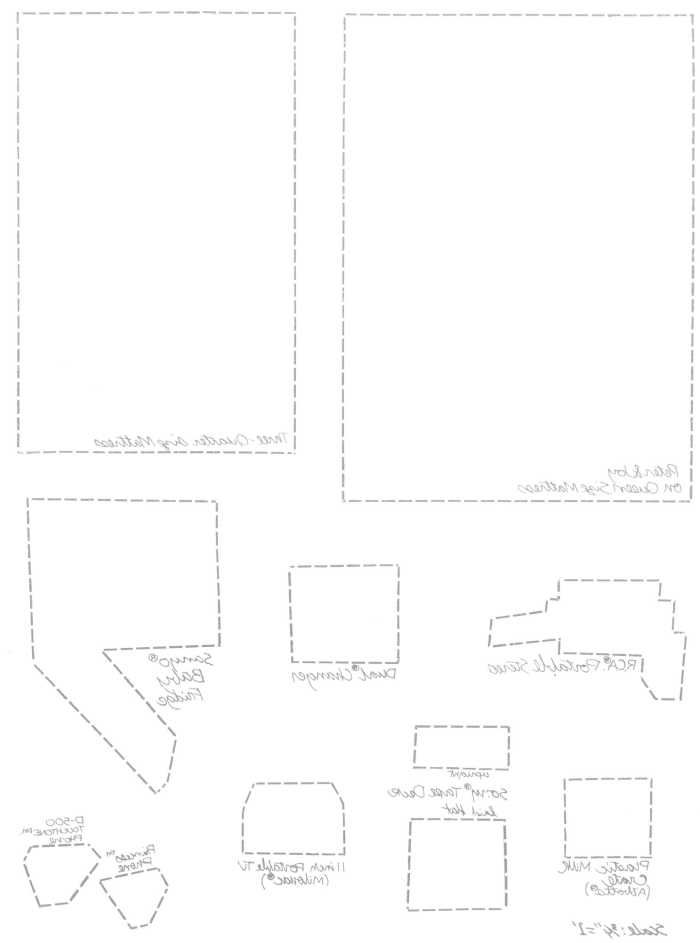

MATTRESS & FURNISHINGS CUTOUTS

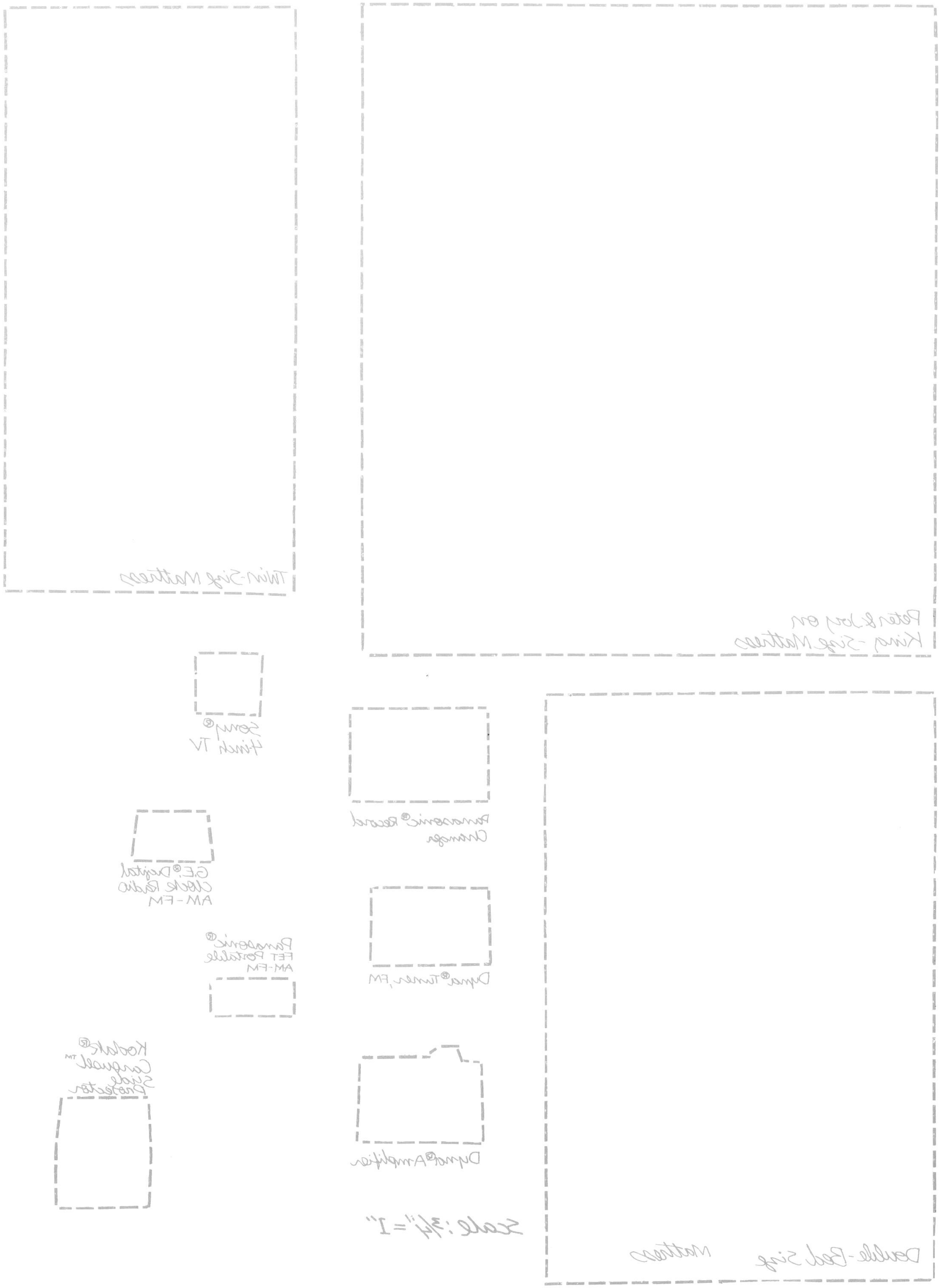

Twin-Size Mattress

Peter & Jon Orr
King-Size Mattress

Sony®
Trinitron TV

Panasonic® Record

Panasonic®
FET Portable
AM-FM

Dynaco® Tuner, FM

Kodak®
Carousel™
Slide
Projector

Dynaco® Amplifier

Scale: 3/4" = 1'

Peter & Joy on
King-Size Mattress

Twin-Size Mattress

Double-Bed Size   Mattress

Panasonic® Record
Changer

Dyna® Tuner, FM

Dyna® Amplifier

Scale : ¾" = 1"

Sony®
4 inch TV

G.E.® Digital
Clock Radio
AM-FM

Panasonic®
FET Portable
AM-FM

Kodak®
Carousel™
Slide
Projector

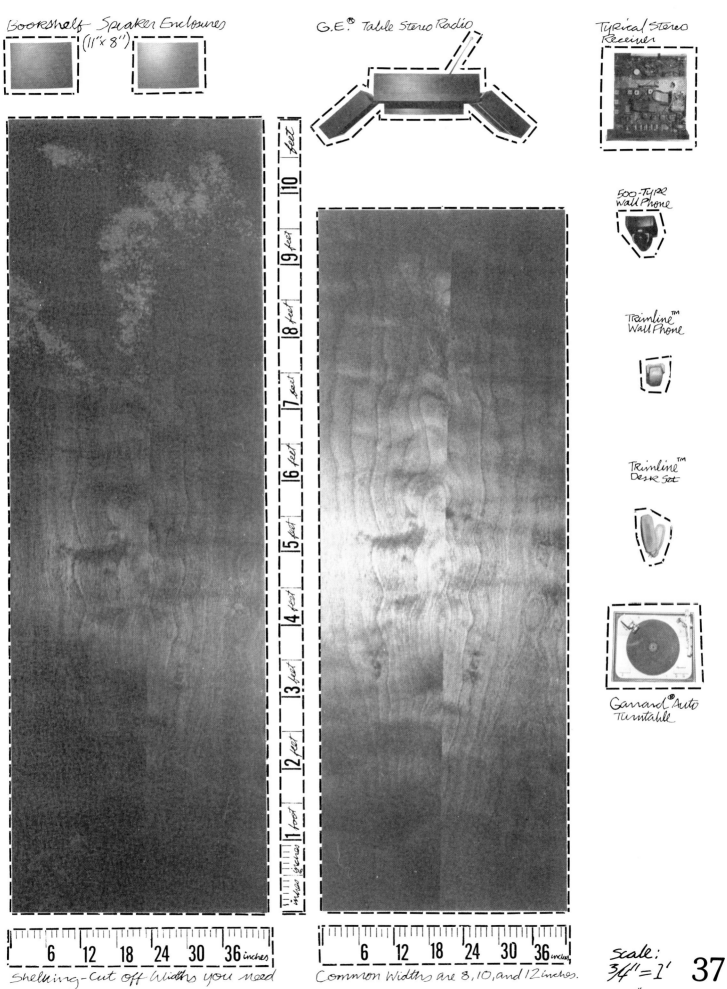

Bookshelf Speaker Enclosures
(11" x 8")

G.E.® Table Stereo Radio

Typical Stereo Receiver

500-Type Wall Phone

Trimline™ Wall Phone

Trimline™ Desk Set

Garrard® Auto Turntable

10 feet

9 feet

8 feet

7 feet

6 feet

5 feet

4 feet

3 feet

2 feet

1 foot

inches

6 12 18 24 30 36 inches

Shelving - Cut off Widths you need

6 12 18 24 30 36 inches

Common Widths are 8, 10, and 12 inches.

Scale:
3/4" = 1'   37

YOU CAN CUT OUT THESE MEASURES & USE THEM FOR PLANNING IN 3/4" SCALE...

Chapter 3
Drywall Basics

Drywall or stick-built, balloon frame; whatever you want to call it, is the most widely used wall building method on the North American Continent. It's acceptance is based upon two factors, an abundance of relatively inexpensive wood and the standardized production of modern lumber mills. Almost the entire homebuilding industry uses this pattern. All frame houses are based on the 8 foot 2 x 4 lumber module. The other element is the distance of 16 inches between the vertical members (studs). It is one of the cheapest possible ways of enclosing space. Even in large buildings that have much stronger and more massive outer structures the inner partitioning is usually drywall.

Combined with gypsum wallboard, the lowly 2 x 4 attains a monolithic visual mass without great weight. It provides the builder with tremendous satisfaction when finished, and is a very simple thing to construct. Even a rank amateur can build a wall using this method and basic tools.

It is for these reasons that I recommend drywall as a loft building medium. All of the permanent loft designs in this book are based on it. After you build a drywall loft, and see how easy it is to do, you'll want to build a house.

The following is a basic manual of Drywall Construction. Only the scale is different. Since a loft is a smaller structure than a house and doesn't need to bear a roof, I've specified 2 x 3's instead of 2 x 4's in many places. I've also specified 24″ between stud centers for the same reason. This uses less material, yet still fits the 4 foot wide panel module.

My drawings will tell most of the story, I'll just add notes when needed.

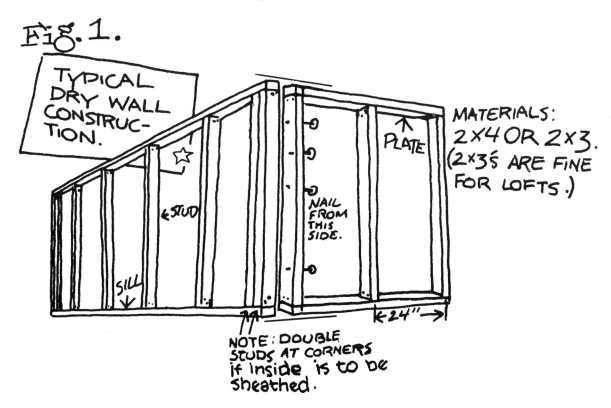

FIG. 1
It may seem strange that two identical members have different names ("sill" and "plate"). When a house is built this way, two 2 x 4's would be used for the top horizontal member. In that case, the plate would be double thickness. The drawing shows the frames as they are raised into place, having been nailed together while lying flat on the floor. After the sections are nailed, the sill is nailed to the floor.

Use double studs at the corners, not for strength, but to provide something on the inside corner to nail wallboard to. It's only needed if you want to sheetrock the inside.

DRYWALL LOFT BUILDING

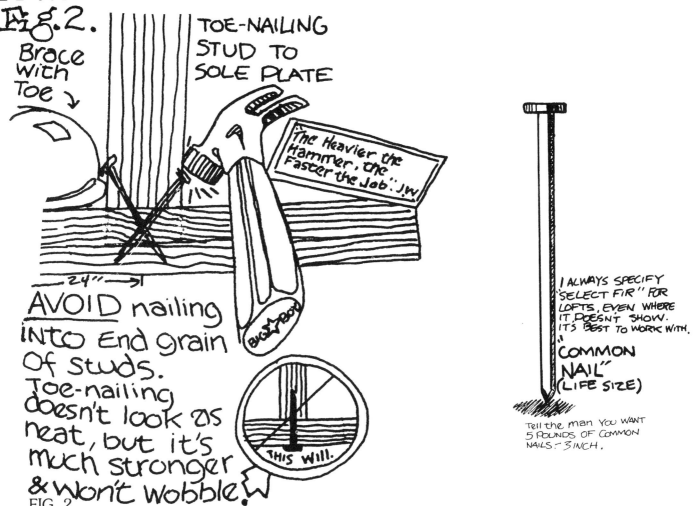

Fig.2. Brace with Toe ↓

TOE-NAILING STUD TO SOLE PLATE

"The Heavier the Hammer, the Faster the Job." J.W.

←— 24" —→

AVOID nailing into end grain of studs. Toe-nailing doesn't look as neat, but it's much stronger & won't wobble!

THIS WILL.

I ALWAYS SPECIFY "SELECT FIR" FOR LOFTS, EVEN WHERE IT DOESN'T SHOW. IT'S BEST TO WORK WITH.

"COMMON NAIL" (LIFE SIZE)

Tell the man you want 5 POUNDS OF COMMON NAILS — 3 INCH.

FIG. 2

You can nail into the stud endgrain as a convenience to locate the studs at 24" on center, then put a nail through the sill and plate to help keep them in place while you're toenailing the lot of them. As you can see in the drawing, the toes of your feet are used to backstop the piece you're nailing. These frame sections are so light there's no mass to resist hammer blows. So, unless you have a wall as a backstop, use your feet.

Fig.3 JOISTS ARE NAILED INTO STRINGERS AT EVERY STUD LOCATION. JOISTS SUPPORT PLYWOOD DECK & HOLD WALLS TOGETHER AT TOP.

(A)

STUD   JOIST   PLATE

BRACE

STRINGER

STUD

SILL →

39

Drywall

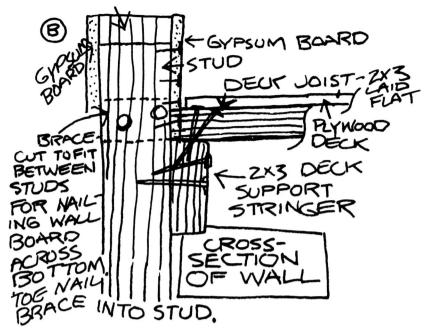

B

GYPSUM BOARD STUD

DECK JOIST-2X3 LAID FLAT

PLYWOOD DECK

2X3 DECK SUPPORT STRINGER

BRACE CUT TO FIT BETWEEN STUDS FOR NAILING WALL BOARD ACROSS BOTTOM TOE NAIL BRACE INTO STUD.

CROSS-SECTION OF WALL

FIG. 3

(A & B) This drawing illustrates the nailing of a joist to the stringer. By using this method, you can achieve a thinner deck; therefore more headroom underneath. The braces between studs are necessary because the gypsum sheathing would be unsupported at the deck and could be pushed inward between the studs. The braces add integrity to the panel.

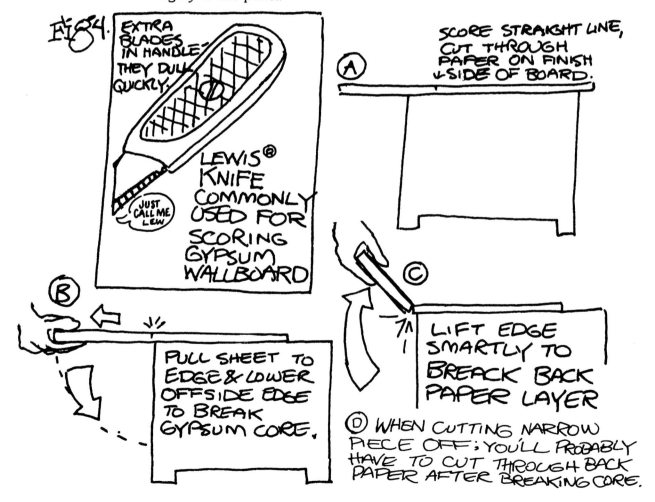

FIG 4.

EXTRA BLADES IN HANDLE- THEY DULL QUICKLY.

LEWIS® KNIFE COMMONLY USED FOR SCORING GYPSUM WALLBOARD

JUST CALL ME LEW

SCORE STRAIGHT LINE, CUT THROUGH PAPER ON FINISH SIDE OF BOARD.

A

B PULL SHEET TO EDGE & LOWER OFFSIDE EDGE TO BREAK GYPSUM CORE.

C LIFT EDGE SMARTLY TO BREAK BACK PAPER LAYER

D WHEN CUTTING NARROW PIECE OFF; YOU'LL PROBABLY HAVE TO CUT THROUGH BACK PAPER AFTER BREAKING CORE.

FIG. 4

Cutting sheetrock is as simple as the drawings. Just be sure that the line is squarely marked and use a metal straightedge if you have unsteady hands. You'll get the hang of it very quickly.

Drywall

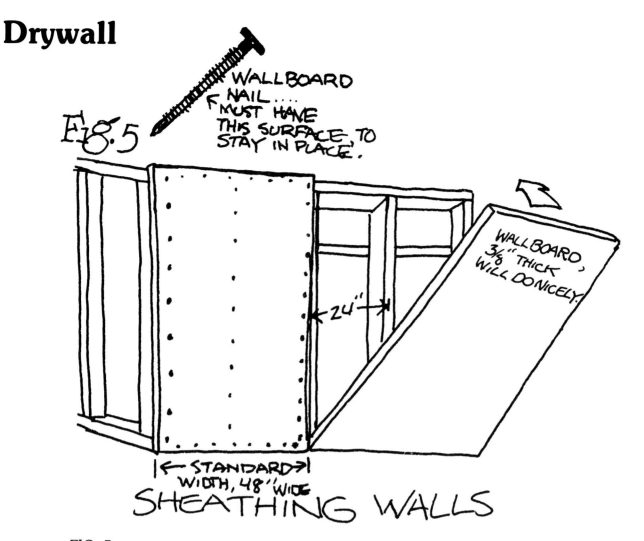

FIG. 5

After cutting panels to length, just put them into place and nail them up, as shown in Fig. 6.

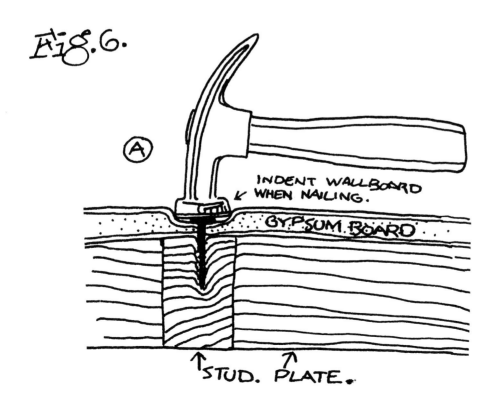

Drywall

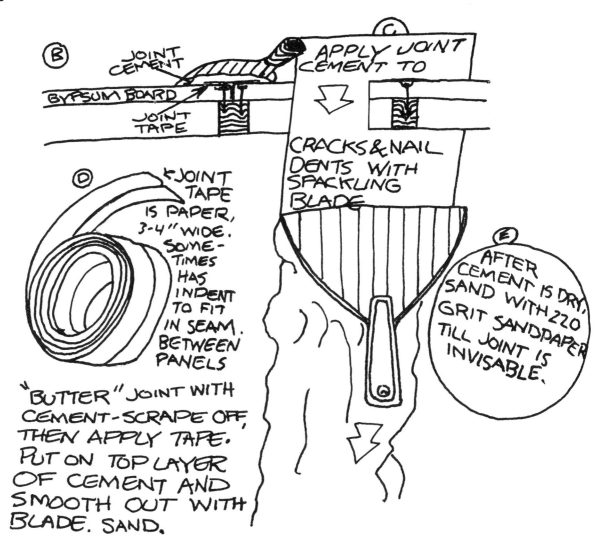

Ⓑ JOINT CEMENT
GYPSUM BOARD
JOINT TAPE

Ⓒ APPLY JOINT CEMENT TO CRACKS & NAIL DENTS WITH SPACKLING BLADE

Ⓓ ←JOINT TAPE IS PAPER, 3-4" WIDE. SOMETIMES HAS INDENT TO FIT IN SEAM. BETWEEN PANELS

Ⓔ AFTER CEMENT IS DRY, SAND WITH 220 GRIT SANDPAPER TILL JOINT IS INVISABLE.

"BUTTER" JOINT WITH CEMENT-SCRAPE OFF, THEN APPLY TAPE. PUT ON TOP LAYER OF CEMENT AND SMOOTH OUT WITH BLADE. SAND.

FIG. 6

If you indent the nail it is less likely to work its way out and makes finishing with joint cement possible (buy a couple of gallon cans of joint cement when you buy the wallboard).

The spackling blade shown in part C should be 4 to 6 inches wide, the wider the better. The tape shown in D is soft and felt textured. Buy a roll with your other materials.

The sanding is to take off the high places and feather the edge into the wall surface (E). After sanding, you may notice low spots. Smooth on some more joint cement and sand again when dry.

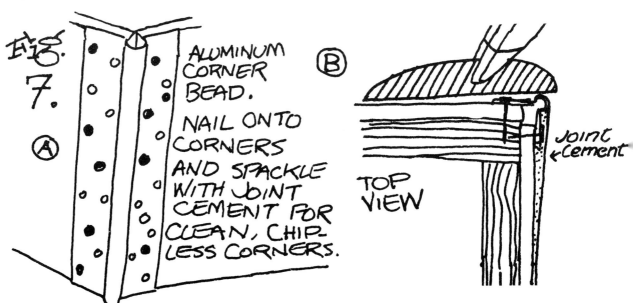

FIG. 7.

Ⓐ ALUMINUM CORNER BEAD. NAIL ONTO CORNERS AND SPACKLE WITH JOINT CEMENT FOR CLEAN, CHIPLESS CORNERS.

Ⓑ TOP VIEW   Joint Cement →

42

Drywall

FIG. 7

Aluminum corner Bead! I really love this stuff. It makes easy to get, beautiful, hardedge corners. You can find it at lumber supply houses and hardware stores. Cut it to length with tin snips or strong scissors that you're not fond of.

Fig. 8.

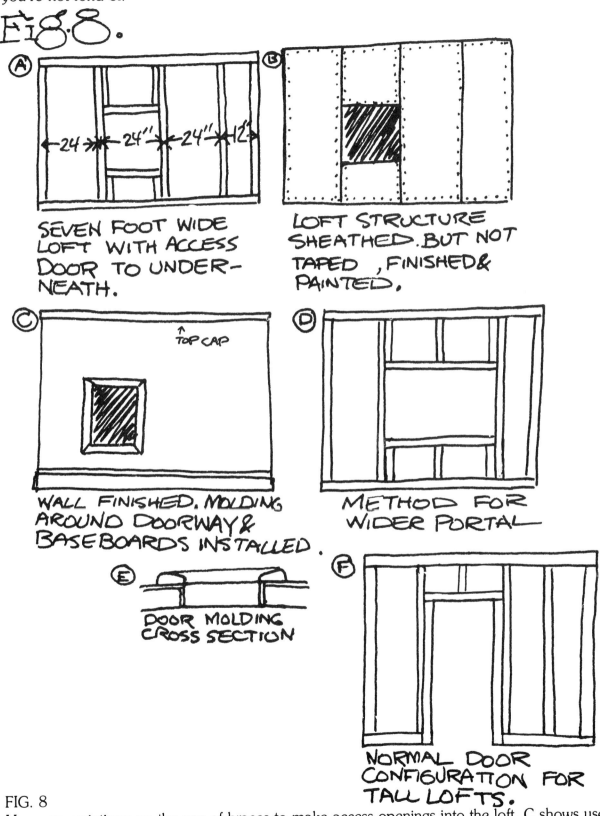

(A) SEVEN FOOT WIDE LOFT WITH ACCESS DOOR TO UNDER-NEATH.

←24→ 24" ←24"→ 12"

(B) LOFT STRUCTURE SHEATHED. BUT NOT TAPED, FINISHED & PAINTED.

(C) WALL FINISHED. MOLDING AROUND DOORWAY & BASEBOARDS INSTALLED.

↑TOP CAP

(D) METHOD FOR WIDER PORTAL

(E) DOOR MOLDING CROSS SECTION

(F) NORMAL DOOR CONFIGURATION FOR TALL LOFTS.

FIG. 8

Here are variations on the use of braces to make access openings into the loft. C shows use of door molding around opening. You may prefer to use corner bead around the edges of the opening, inside and out. When finished and painted it'll look like the hole was sliced out very cleanly.

Drywall

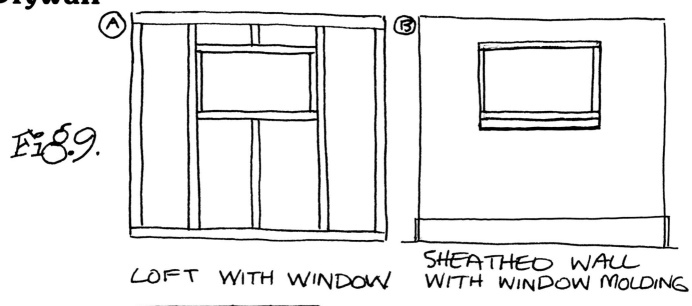

Fig. 9.

Ⓐ LOFT WITH WINDOW.

Ⓑ SHEATHED WALL WITH WINDOW MOLDING

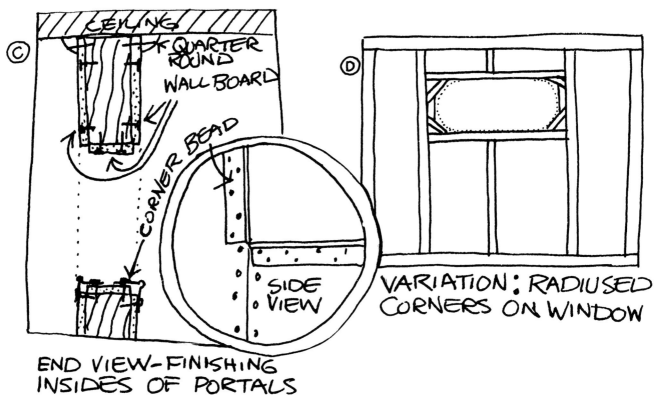

Ⓒ CEILING
QUARTER ROUND
WALLBOARD
CORNER BEAD
SIDE VIEW
END VIEW-FINISHING INSIDES OF PORTALS

Ⓓ VARIATION: RADIUSED CORNERS ON WINDOW

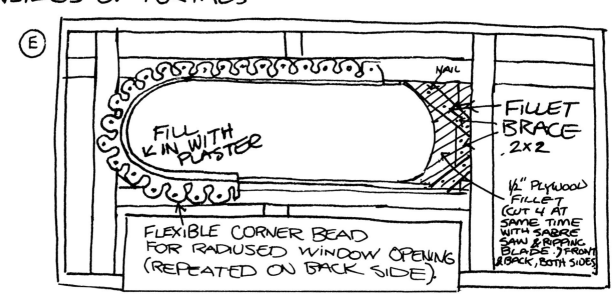

Ⓔ FILL IN WITH PLASTER

NAIL

FILLET BRACE .2x2

½" PLYWOOD FILLET (CUT 4 AT SAME TIME WITH SABRE SAW & RIPPING BLADE.) FRONT & BACK, BOTH SIDES

FLEXIBLE CORNER BEAD FOR RADIUSED WINDOW OPENING (REPEATED ON BACK SIDE).

44

Drywall

FIG. 9
By doing a near-ceiling height loft wall you can work in window openings. This makes for a very cozy loft. If you ever had a thing about **The House at Pooh Corner**, this is where you can plug into your fantasy. Flexible corner bead opens up further possibilities (D). How about a perfect circle? You can do it with this. Of course the frame of the wall gets a little complicated, but with time and a lot of plaster it's no big deal.

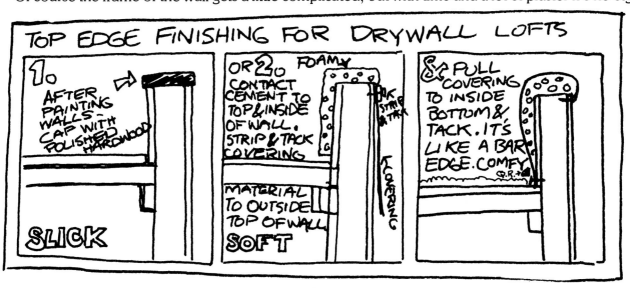

FIG. 10

Baseboard molding is good for making a nice division between a wall and a floor. If you want to do one, this is a good, simple design to use. You may get other ideas from looking at molding samples at a lumber yard. You'll need a mitre box and saw, but once you have them, you'll be able to cut picture frame molding. Box and saw combinations range in price from ten to fifty dollars. You get what you pay for.

Drywall

Other things to consider: gypsum board comes in 8, 10 and 12 foot lengths. If your loft wall is five feet high, you ought to get 10 foot long sheetrock. It makes for fewer cuts and less patching of panels. Remember: every horizontal seam has to be braced or it'll break open.

The same thing applies to lumber. It usually comes in 8, 10, and 12 foot lengths. Good planning means a lot less waste.

You should consult the wiring chapter after you have erected the frames. It's much easier to do the job at this point. All you have to do then is cut holes for outlets while fitting panels.

Textured paint makes for an interesting loft skin. It's a special latex paint with sand in it. You glop it on thickly, and swirl it around with a broom. Then paint it with white latex paint. Don't stipple it with a sponge though, as it will have little sharp teeth when dry.

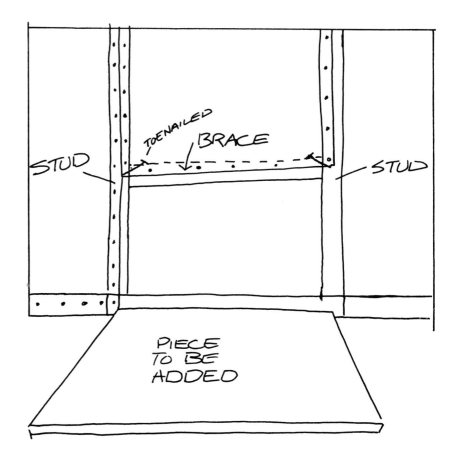

Chapter 4

B.T.L. Fasteners

BASIC CONSTRUCTION
PRINCIPLES OF BOLT-TOGETHER LOFTS

Most bolt-together lofts use four basic fastening devices. They each have specific functions. The need determines which fastener to use.

The carriage bolt (Fig. 1. & 2) comes in various lengths and diameters. I normally use 3/8" or 1/4" in 4 inch lengths, sometimes longer. They are very convenient fasteners to use, only one wrench is needed to tighten them. When used in a hole only slightly larger than the shaft of the bolt, the tang holds the bolt immobile as the nut is turned. The broad mushroom head resists wobbling without need of a washer,

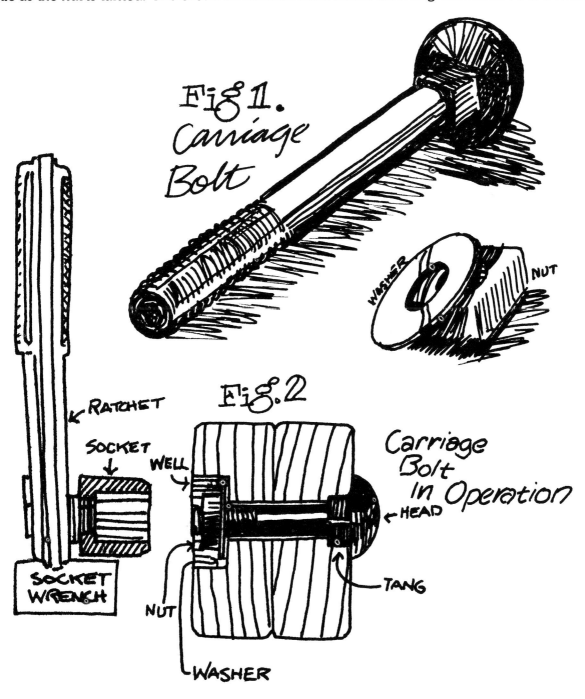

Fig 1. Carriage Bolt

WASHER   NUT

RATCHET

SOCKET

WELL

SOCKET WRENCH

Fig. 2

Carriage Bolt In Operation

HEAD

TANG

NUT

WASHER

BASIC CONSTRUCTION
PRINCIPLES OF BOLT-TOGETHER LOFTS

although a washer is used under the nut. It's function is to reduce friction, broaden the compression area of the nut, and prevent the nut from digging itself into the wood. If you want the nut to be below surface level, drill a larger hole about 3/4″ deep (Fig. 3.) to accomodate the nut and the socket of the tightening wrench. Be sure to pick a bolt which is shorter than the width of the combined pieces being bolted together. For added sleekness, cut a thin slice from a wooden dowel the same size as the bolt well (Fig. 4). After the nut is tightened, put glue on the walls of the well and the side of the plug. Then, force the plug in flush with the surface. After the glue is set, sand the surface smooth.

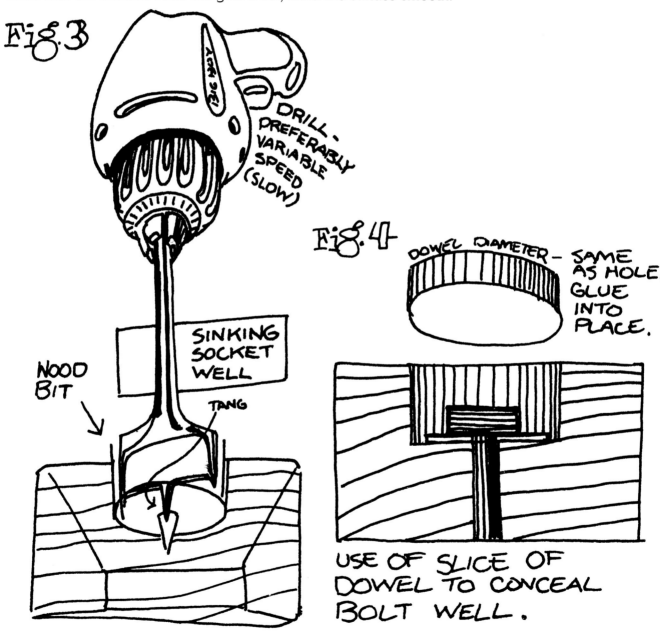

Fig. 3

DRILL - PREFERABLY VARIABLE SPEED (SLOW)

SINKING SOCKET WELL

WOOD BIT

TANG

Fig. 4

DOWEL DIAMETER - SAME AS HOLE. GLUE INTO PLACE.

USE OF SLICE OF DOWEL TO CONCEAL BOLT WELL.

BOLT-TOGETHER LOFTS

Fig. 5
Ordinary Bolt
NUT
WASHER

The ordinary bolt (Fig. 5) is used in these lofts only when it isn't possible to turn the nut. This happens in the leg fastening method seen in Fig. 6., and is the neatest way I've developed for holding a post to an overhead member. It acts as a reverse carriage bolt. A 5/8″ diameter hole is bored into the center of the post. Then another hole, this one a little larger than the width of the nut, is drilled through the side of the post intersecting the vertical hole. The bolt (I normally use 1/2″ diameter bolts for this job) with washer on

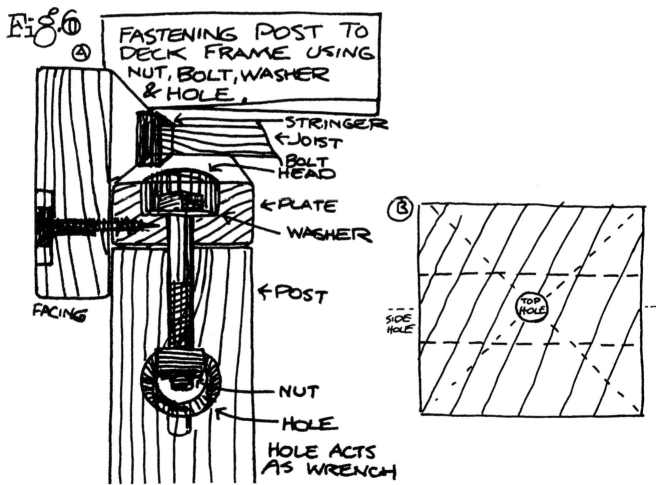

Fig. 6

(A) FASTENING POST TO DECK FRAME USING NUT, BOLT, WASHER & HOLE.

STRINGER
JOIST
BOLT HEAD
PLATE
WASHER
POST
NUT
HOLE
HOLE ACTS AS WRENCH

FACING

(B)
SIDE HOLE
TOP HOLE

top is dropped into the hole through the plate and post. Hold the nut in place with your fingers while its head is turned to start the threads. As soon as the bolt is tight enough to prevent the bolt head from turning stick a screwdriver into the side hole between the nut and the hole wall. Then gently turn the head with a wrench. After the nut has sunk a bit into the wood, you can apply stronger wrench pressure until the plate and the post are immovable.

BOLT-TOGETHER LOFTS

With diagonal bracing, you have a light, simple, very rigid leg structure. Fig. 7 shows the simplest way I've found to flush mount a diagonal brace to a post. This method uses the lag screw (Fig. 8) as a fastener.

The lag screw is basically a large screw with a heavy, square head for use with a wrench. As shown in Fig. 7B, the well is drilled at a 90° angle to the post. After it reaches the proper depth, switch to a drill bit smaller than the threads of the screw (Fig. 9). Next drill through the brace and into the post. Again, a washer is used under the nut.

The flat head wood screw (Fig. 10) is used to fasten a relatively thin board down.

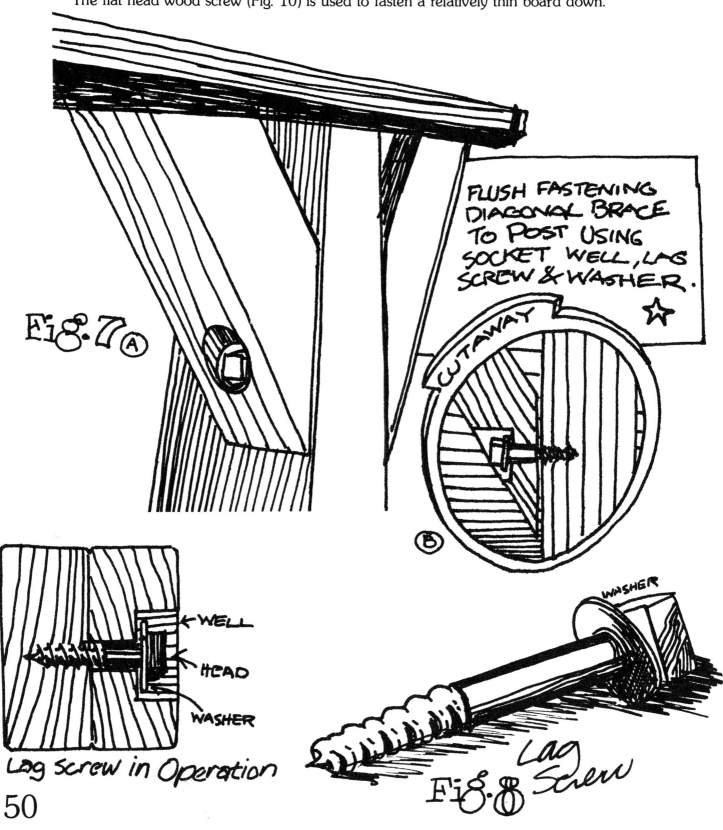

Fig. 7 A

FLUSH FASTENING DIAGONAL BRACE TO POST USING SOCKET WELL, LAG SCREW & WASHER. ☆

CUTAWAY

B

WELL
HEAD
WASHER

Lag Screw in Operation

WASHER

Fig. 8 Lag Screw

Nails are used occasionally, especially when building sub-assemblies that aren't to be taken apart. I normally use Elmer's glue between the pieces and nail them with finishing nails (Fig. 11). A finishing nail is a nail with a small head that has a dimple in the center. The nail is driven till the head is almost flush with the surface, then a punch is used to drive it below the surface. This leaves an inconspicuous hole that is easily filled, creating a smooth wood surface. The finishing nail serves only to hold the two pieces under

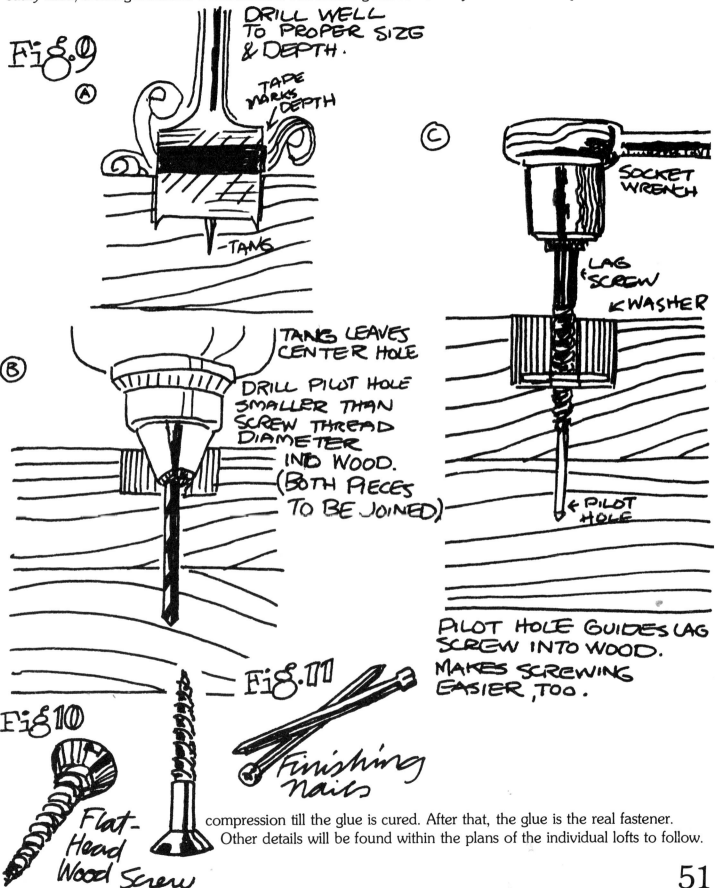

Fig. 9

(A) DRILL WELL TO PROPER SIZE & DEPTH.

TAPE MARKS DEPTH

TANG

(B) TANG LEAVES CENTER HOLE

DRILL PILOT HOLE SMALLER THAN SCREW THREAD DIAMETER INTO WOOD. (BOTH PIECES TO BE JOINED)

(C) SOCKET WRENCH

LAG SCREW & WASHER

PILOT HOLE

PILOT HOLE GUIDES LAG SCREW INTO WOOD. MAKES SCREWING EASIER, TOO.

Fig 10

Flat-Head Wood Screw

Fig. 11

Finishing Nails

compression till the glue is cured. After that, the glue is the real fastener. Other details will be found within the plans of the individual lofts to follow.

Bolt-Together Loft

A bolt-together loft is constructed in such a way as to permit it to be disassembled easily for moving. The initial cost for this type of loft may be slightly higher than for the permanent loft, but if you don't plan to live in your present location more than a couple of years, you will save money because you can take it with you to your new place.

In general, you will have to be more careful of your workmanship with a bolt-together loft, as there is usually no skin covering the structure.

It's possible that you will want to build this type of loft only for the reason of the more "wooden" look to it. The bolt-together loft has more of a furniture character, while the permanent loft becomes a part of the room architecture.

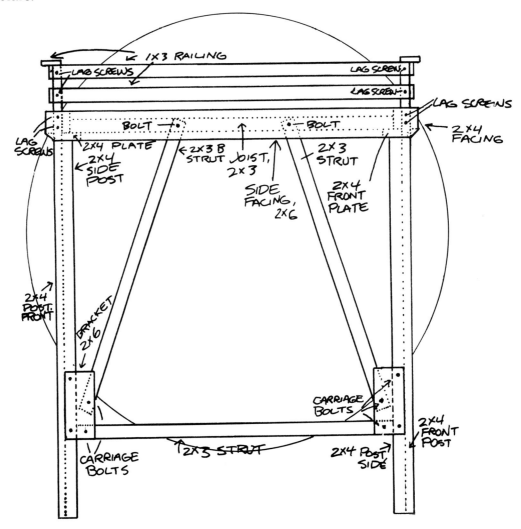

Permanent Loft

Permanent lofts have several advantages over bolt-together lofts. Although they may have more structural members, therefore more sawing, assembly is basically hammer-and-nail. There is usually no drilling and cutting at angles involved. This means that much less woodworking skill is needed, and the project therefore is more easily handled by the novice carpenter.

Tools required for this type of loft are minimal. What you'll need will be: a circular cutoff saw, a good heavy hammer, a level, a tape measure, a carpenter's square and a knife. A handsaw can be used in place of the circular saw, it's just slower.

Don't be misled by the term "permanent". All the materials in this type of loft can be reused except the paneling material; it's usually destroyed by disassembly. This is especially true of gypsum board. If you go to move your loft, a nail puller will be very handy.

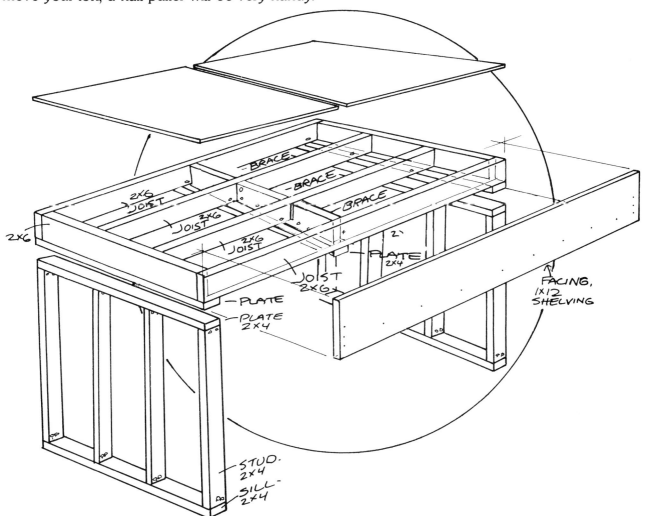

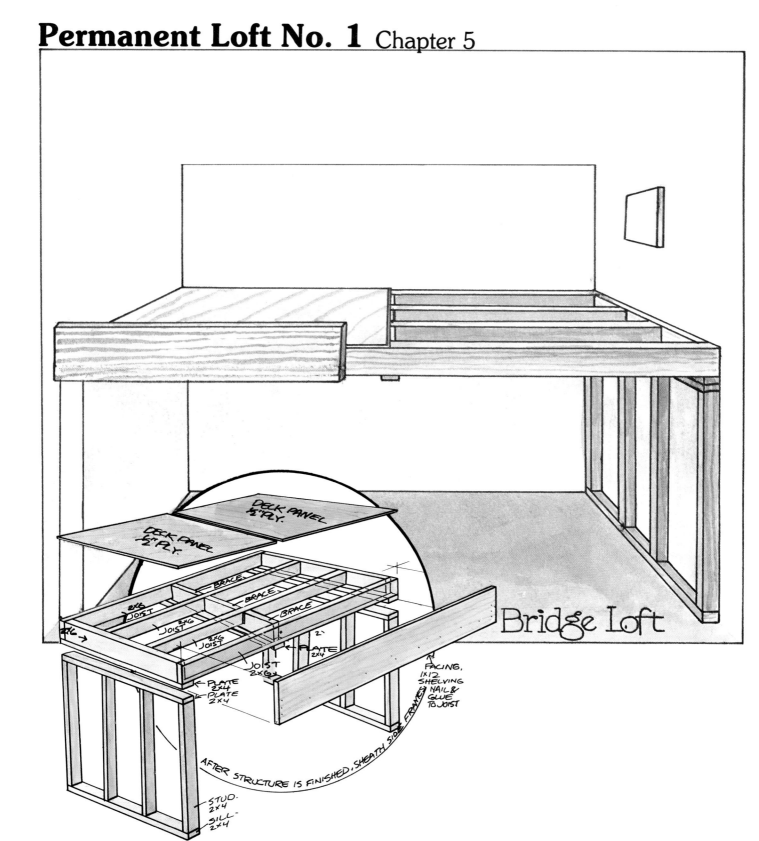

DECK PANEL ½" PLY.

DECK PANEL ½" PLY.

BRACE

BRACE

BRACE

2X6 JOIST

JOIST 2X6

2X6 JOIST

2X6

2X6 →

JOIST 2X6

PLATE 2X4

2'

PLATE 2X4

PLATE 2X4

1" FACING, 1X12 SHELVING NAIL & GLUE TO JOIST

AFTER STRUCTURE IS FINISHED, SHEATH SIDE FRAMES

STUD. 2X4

SILL 2X4

Bridge Loft

BRIDGE LOFT

Here is a hybrid design. It has features of both the permanent and bolt-together types. It's perfect if you have an 8 to 12 foot wide alcove, or high-ceilinged hallway. The deck structure is made up of 2 x 6's for strength and is supported by the drywall side frames. These, as well as the deck sides, should be attached to the wall by masonry spikes or wall anchors as a safety precaution. Actually, once the deck is attached to the side frames and they are nailed to the floor it should be stable enough. Try it and see, you may be perfectly happy with it without the wall mounting.

Any-type ladder will work well with this design.

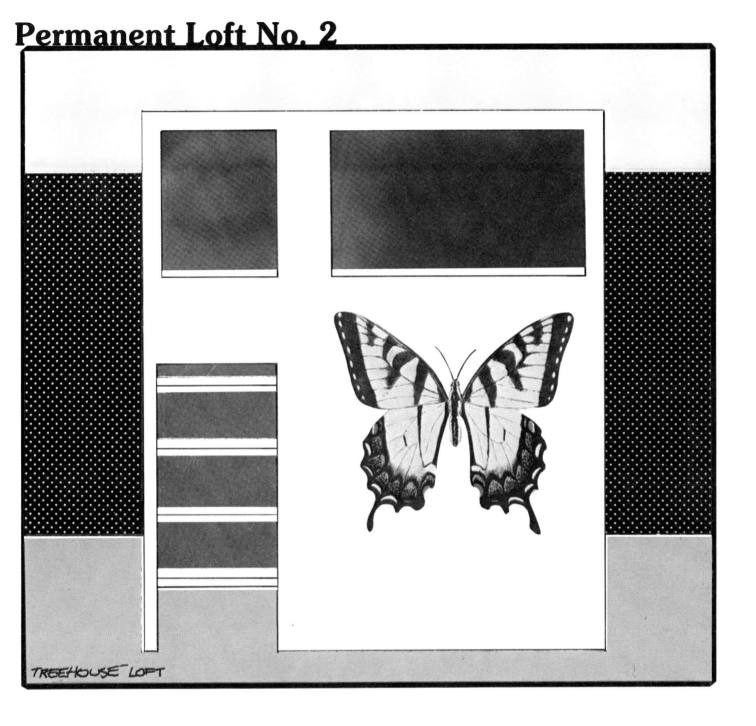

TREEHOUSE LOFT

TREEHOUSE LOFT

If you have the ceiling height and room space, this will be a terrific loft to build. A minimum height of 12 feet for the ceiling is necessary, which limits its use. But, this is definitely the loft for an industrial studio space.

Although the size is huge, it's still just simple drywall construction, so don't be afraid to try it.

Because of its enclosed nature, the treehouse is probably the best for acoustic designing. The drywall construction allows you to incorporate poly-planar speakers into the walls (see sound chapter for plans).

You may want to work a ventilation blower into it to help air circulation if you like to keep the windows closed.

The space underneath lends itself very naturally for use as a bathroom or small kitchen. That optional area can become an important quality when faced with an industrial space that lacks either of those rooms.

Permanent Loft No. 2

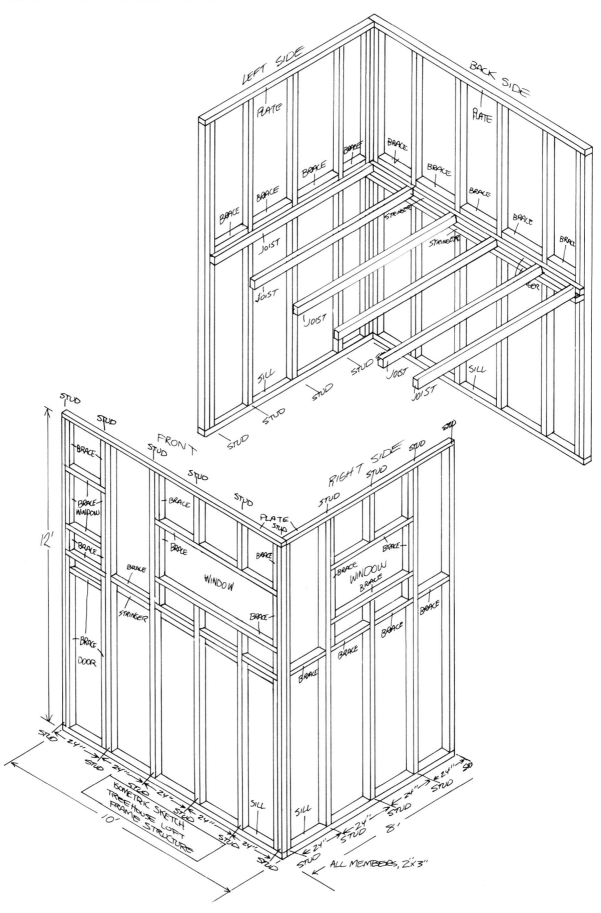

Permanent Loft No. 1

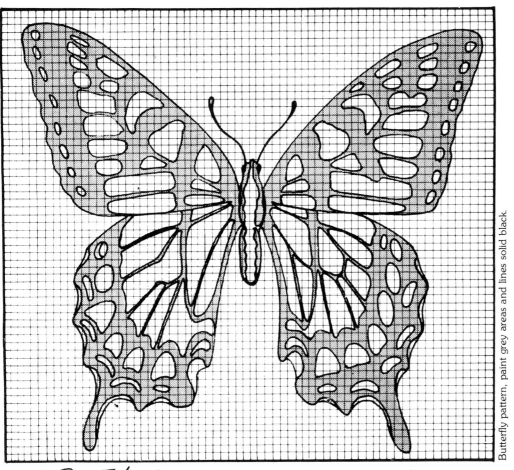

Butterfly pattern, paint grey areas and lines solid black.

Wall Butterfly Pattern each grid square = 1"
Pencil grid on wall and transfer design to Grid.

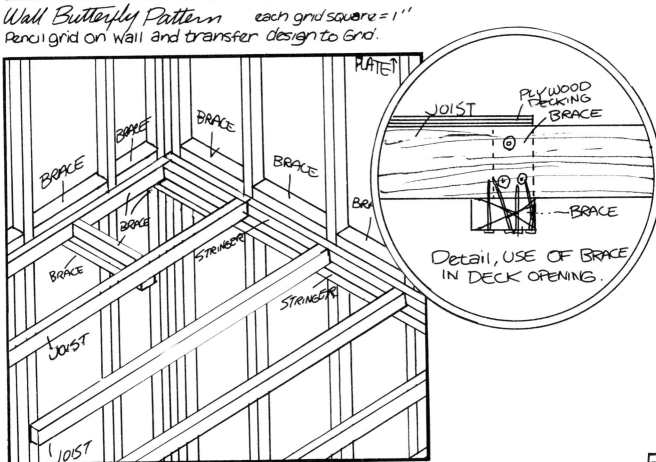

Detail, USE OF BRACE IN DECK OPENING.

Bolt-Together Loft No. 1

AZTEC ELEVATOR

BUILD IT IN A FEW HOURS FOR 50.00
SAND IT, SHELLAC IT, AND PAINT IT SILVER.

Bolt-Together Loft No. 2

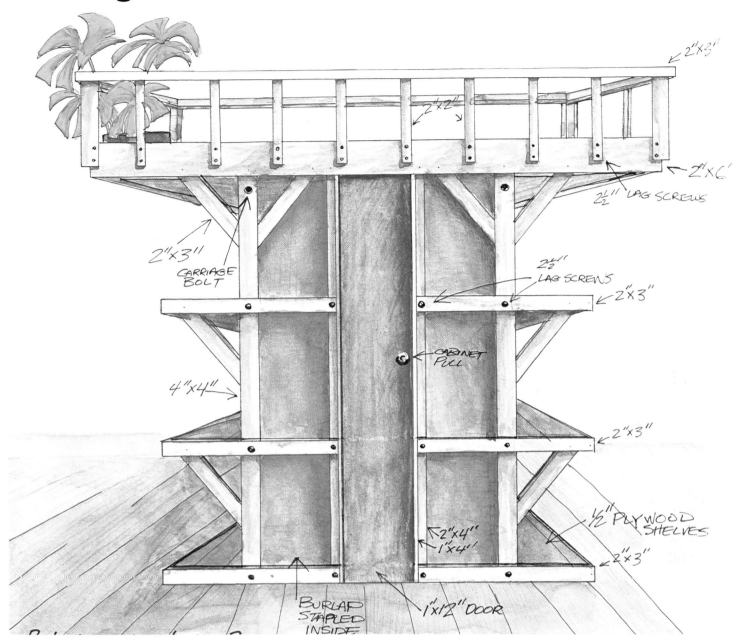

2"x3"

2"x2"

2"x6"

2½" LAG SCREWS

2"x3"
CARRIAGE
BOLT

2½" LAG SCREWS

2"x3"

CABINET
PULL

4"x4"

2"x3"

½" PLYWOOD
SHELVES

2"x3"

2"x4"
1"x4"

BURLAP
STAPLED
INSIDE

1"x12" DOOR

CLOSET LOFT

This one was designed for my friend Pete who had the problem of a small apartment with low ceilings and a shortage of storage space. As it is shown in the drawing, the height is 7'2" to the top of the railing, however, the height can be changed to fit the room ceiling height (see loft planning kit for loft headroom needs). Deck height should be at least 4'6" if you plan to utilize the closet space. The distance between shelves is also a variable, depending on what you plan to put on them.

Although this loft uses five fewer posts than B-T. L #1, at equal height it will cost about the same. This is due to the 2' × 3''s and plywood needed for the shelf structure. The door to the closet is an option, but if the storage space under your loft is as packed as mine, a door might prevent something from falling out and killing someone. Since the doorway is only twelve inches wide, you can use just about anything to fill it. In the drawing above, I've indicated mahogany, which is fairly common in that width (also cheaper compared to walnut). I've also indicated colored burlap to fill the interstices between posts. You can use wallboard, canvas, nylon, or just about anything that can be removed easily for moving.

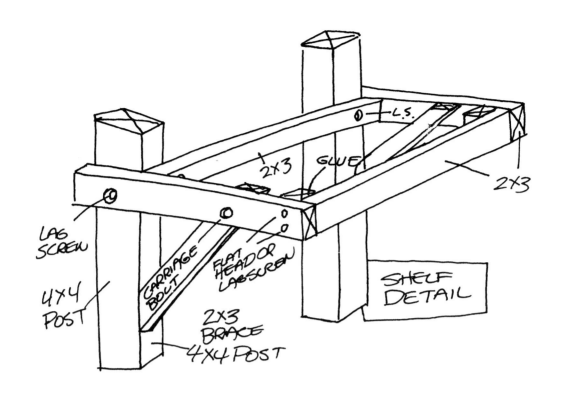

L.S.

2X3

GLUE

2X3

LAG SCREW

CARRIAGE BOLT

FLAT HEAD OR LAGSCREW

4X4 POST

2X3 BRACE

4X4 POST

SHELF DETAIL

PLAN VIEW

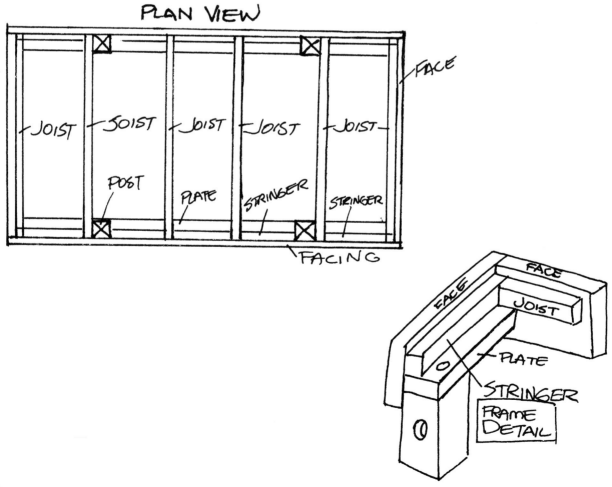

JOIST

JOIST

JOIST

JOIST

JOIST

POST

PLATE

STRINGER

STRINGER

FACE

FACING

FACE

FACE

JOIST

PLATE

STRINGER

FRAME DETAIL

60

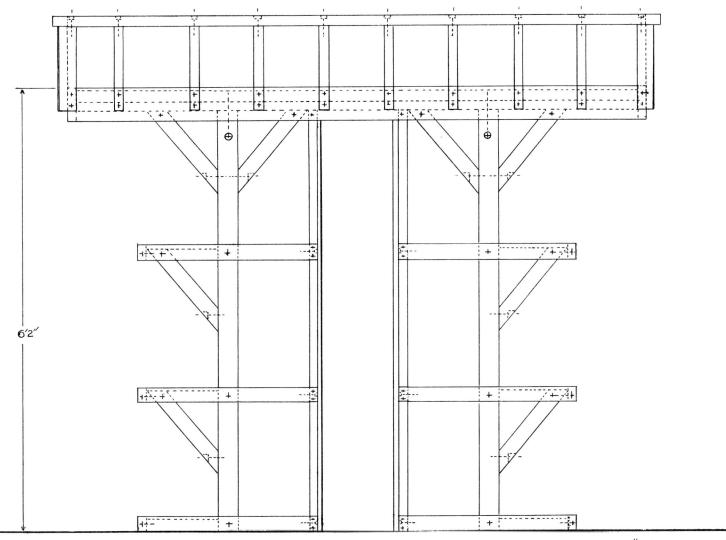

6'2"

Scale: 3/4" = 1'

61

"Say, what kind of loft is this, anyway?"

"A BIG ONE."

BIG LOFT

This loft is almost an extra room. It's a sort of conversation pit in reverse. It will accommodate eight people. The top edge stops a foot short of the ceiling, to allow good air circulation. I recommend the use of soft wall coverings on this one.

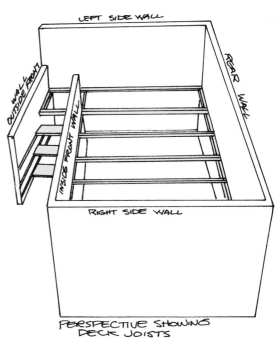

PERSPECTIVE SHOWING
DECK JOISTS

62 UNFOLDED VIEW - BIG LOFT
JOISTS NOT SHOWN

Bolt-Together Loft No.3

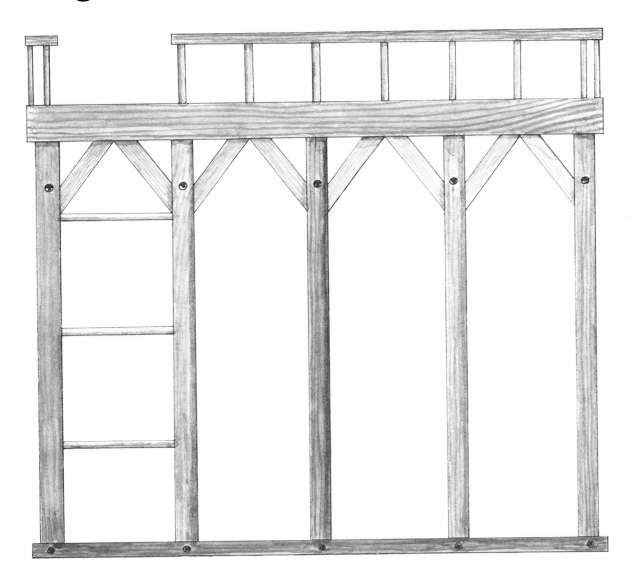

Elizabethan Loft

This loft was designed for a carpenter friend who wanted to get into something a little more exciting than fences. He also was interested in a product that would sell for a lot of money; in this case $1,000.

The construction was stretched out over a three week period, mainly because Carl was leary of working on it when I wasn't there, and also because we would usually guzzle lots of beer to cut the sawdust. By working at a fairly steady pace and staying sober, this loft could have easily been finished in three days.

The loft has nine 4 × 4 supports, five on the front and two more per side. The back side is supported by lag screws connecting the deck to the wall of the room. This saves on materials and gives one unobstructed wall surface for the space underneath. It also makes it simpler to put a sofa under the unit. The large number of posts makes it easier to build in desks, tables, shelves, etc.

This design wastes a lot of material; it would be just as strong with five or six posts. There are drawings a little further on that illustrate these configurations. The large number of struts compensate by creating a very elegant looking structure. It reminds me of a box seat in an Elizabethan theater.

Cost of materials at the end of 1974 was approximately $100.00. This is based on a 4′ × 8′ deck. A larger deck would cost a little more, mostly for additional plywood.

Bolt-Together Loft No. 3

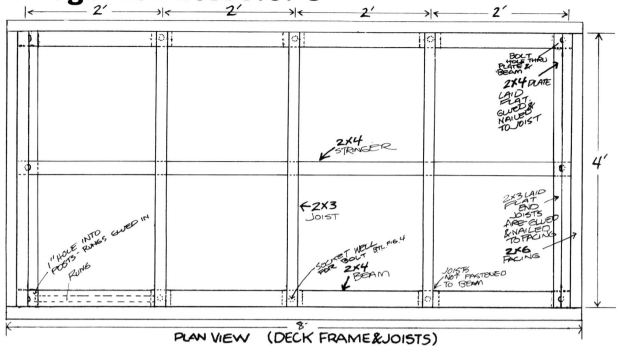

PLAN VIEW (DECK FRAME & JOISTS)

Labels in plan view:
- 2' 2' 2' 2'
- BOLT HOLE THRU PLATE & BEAM
- 2X4 PLATE LAID FLAT GLUED & NAILED TO JOIST
- 4'
- 2X4 STRINGER
- 2X3 LAID FLAT END JOISTS ARE GLUED & NAILED TO FACING
- 2X3 JOIST
- 2X6 FACING
- 1" HOLE INTO POSTS-RUNGS GLUED IN RUNG
- SOCKET WELL FOR BOLT BTL. FIG.4
- 2X4 BEAM
- JOISTS NOT FASTENED TO BEAM
- 8'

note: For larger deck, see Vanity Loft plans pp. 67

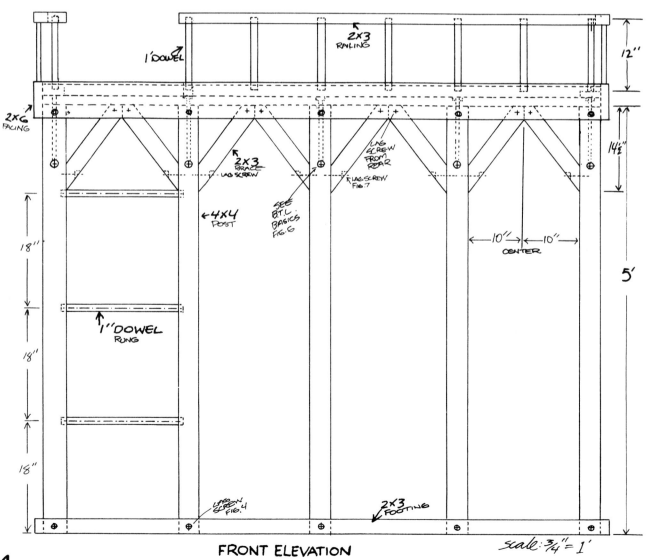

FRONT ELEVATION

Labels in front elevation:
- 2X3 RAILING
- 1' DOWEL
- 12"
- 2X6 FACING
- 14½"
- LAG SCREW FROM REAR
- 2X3 BRACE LAG SCREW
- LAG SCREW FIG.7
- SEE B.T.L. BASICS FIG.6
- 4X4 POST
- 5'
- 10" 10" CENTER
- 18"
- 1" DOWEL RUNG
- 18"
- 18"
- LAG SCREW FIG.4
- 2X3 FOOTING
- scale: ¾" = 1'

64

Bolt-Together Loft No. 3

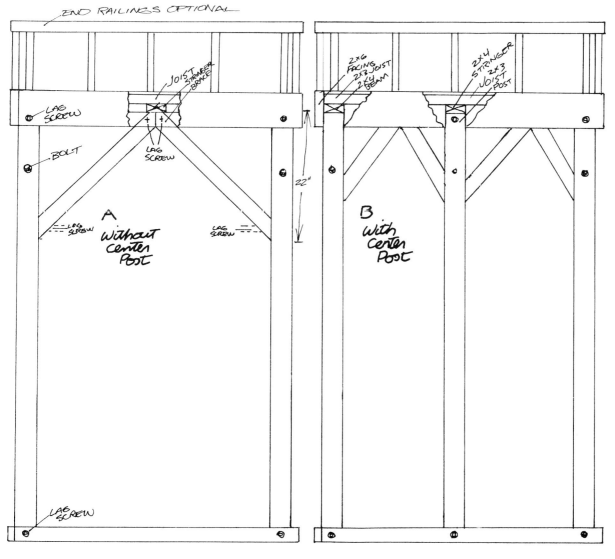

SIDE ELEVATION

65

Bolt-Together
Loft No. 3

Photos by KAS

Bolt-Together Loft No. 4

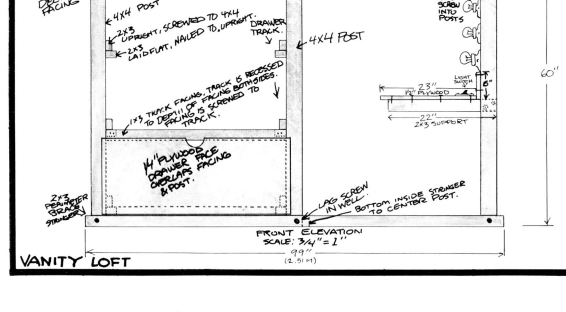

PLAN VIEW

Labels in plan view:
- 96"
- 24" 24" 24" 24"
- 22" 17"
- 2x8 FIXED JOIST
- 2x3
- 2x8 DECK FACING
- 2x3, LAID FLAT, NAILED ON
- 2x4, UPRIGHT, NAILED TO 2x3
- 2x4 LAID FLAT NOT NAILED
- TOP STRINGER CONNECTS CENTER POST TO SIDE POSTS
- 4X4 POST
- LAG SCREW IN WELL INTO POST
- 4X4 POST
- 2X3, UPRIGHT, NAILED TO 2x4
- 4X4 POST
- 2X3 UPRIGHT NAILED TO 2x8
- 2X4 LAID FLAT NAILED TO 2x3
- 2X3 UPRIGHT JOIST NOT NAILED
- 4X4 POST
- 4X4 POST
- 22"
- 63"
- 60"
- 34"

FRONT ELEVATION
SCALE: 3/4" = 1"

Labels in front elevation:
- 1X3 LAID FLAT
- 1X3 UPRIGHT
- 1X3 POST
- SCREWS
- INSIDE STRINGER TO CENTER POST.
- LAG SCREW IN WELL.
- 12"
- 4"
- 2X8 DECK FACING
- 4X4 POST
- 2X3 UPRIGHT, SCREWED TO 4X4
- 2X3 LAID FLAT, NAILED TO UPRIGHT.
- DRAWER TRACK.
- 4X4 POST
- PORCELAIN SOCKETS SCREW INTO POSTS
- 1X3 TRACK FACING, TRACK IS RECESSED TO DEPTH OF FACING BOTH SIDES. FACING IS SCREWED TO TRACK.
- LIGHT SWITCH
- 6"
- 23"
- 1/2" PLYWOOD
- 22" 2X3 SUPPORT
- 60"
- 1/4" PLYWOOD DRAWER FACE OVERLAPS FACING & POST.
- 2X3 PERIMETER BRACE STRINGER
- LAG SCREW IN WELL.
- BOTTOM INSIDE STRINGER TO CENTER POST.
- 99" (2.51 M)

VANITY LOFT

VANITY LOFT

This one was designed for a small bedroom. It combines bed, dresser and makeup table in one unit. There's even a space behind the drawers for hanging clothes.

I have made the drawer and track assembly as simple as possible. There are better ways of designing these parts, but none that lend themselves as easily to hand tool construction. Refer to the wiring section for installing vanity light sockets & wiring. The cheap ceramic sockets are fine for this loft, but you could use fluorescent fixtures or fancier bulb sockets.

Bolt-Together Loft No. 4

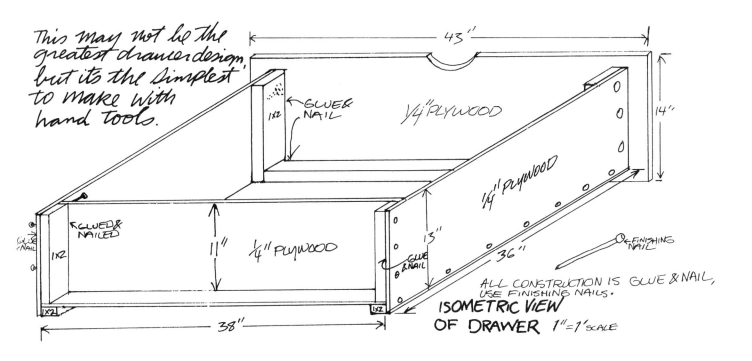

This may not be the greatest drawer design, but its the simplest to make with hand tools.

GLUE & NAIL

1×2

¼" PLYWOOD

14"

¼" PLYWOOD

GLUE & NAILED

1×2

11"

¼" PLYWOOD

13"

36"

GLUE & NAIL

GLUE & NAIL

1×2

FINISHING NAIL

38"

1×2

43"

ALL CONSTRUCTION IS GLUE & NAIL, USE FINISHING NAILS.

ISOMETRIC VIEW OF DRAWER 1"=1' SCALE

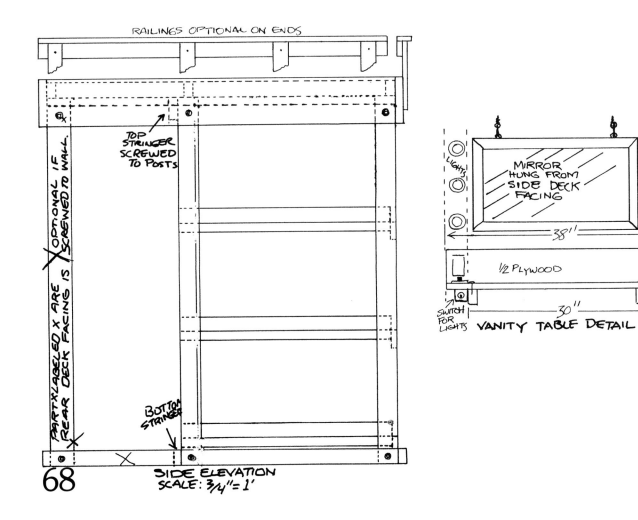

RAILINGS OPTIONAL ON ENDS

TOP STRINGER SCREWED TO POSTS

PARTS LABELED X ARE OPTIONAL IF REAR DECK FACING IS SCREWED TO WALL.

BOTTOM STRINGER

SIDE ELEVATION
SCALE: 3/4" = 1'

MIRROR HUNG FROM SIDE DECK FACING

LIGHTS

LIGHTS

38"

½ PLYWOOD

6"

SWITCH FOR LIGHTS

30"

2×3 SUPPORT LAG SCREWED TO POSTS

VANITY TABLE DETAIL

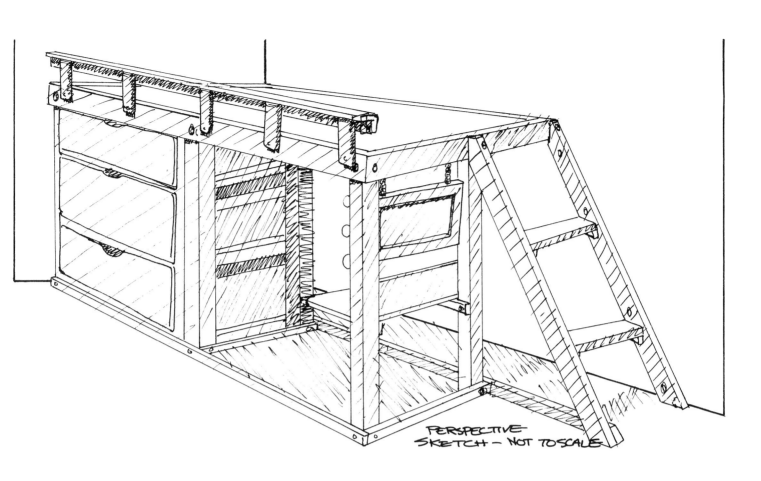

PERSPECTIVE
SKETCH – NOT TO SCALE

Permanent Loft No. 4

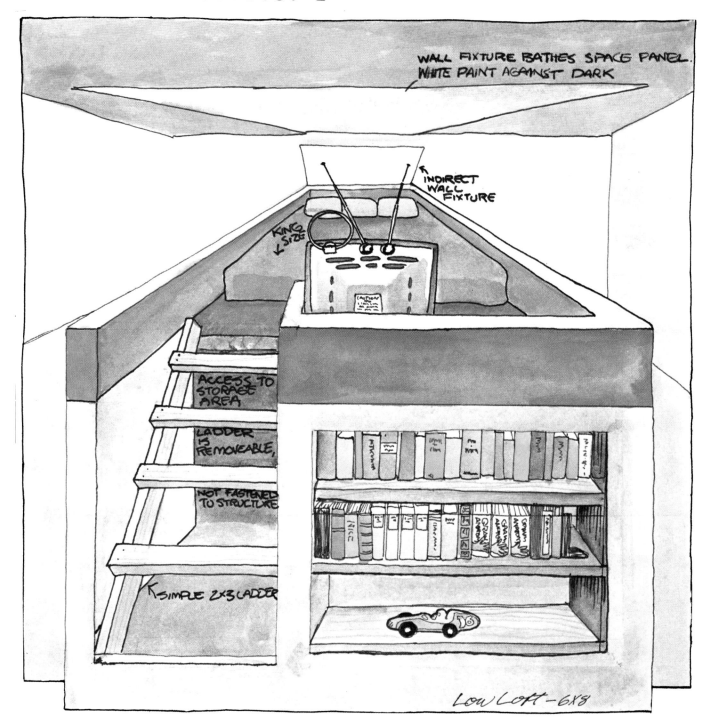

WALL FIXTURE BATHES SPACE PANEL.
WHITE PAINT AGAINST DARK

INDIRECT WALL FIXTURE

KING SIZE

ACCESS TO STORAGE AREA

LADDER IS REMOVEABLE,

NOT FASTENED TO STRUCTURE

SIMPLE 2X3 LADDER

Low Loft — 6X8

LOW LOFT

This design is well suited to rooms with low ceilings. As drawn in the plans, deck height is 3 feet. There is a lot of storage space underneath that is ideal for anything kept in boxes.

I have specified 2 x 4's for the wall structure only because I wanted a thicker wall section. 2 x 3's are certainly strong enough, so use them if you'd prefer; nothing else is changed if you do.

The white ceiling panel is the same size as the loft and it's positioned directly above. The panel, like most other details will work just as well with different loft designs, especially those with indirect lighting. A white ceiling is necessary when using the tricolor loft light.

The built-in bookshelves are an option — use that feature only if you're interested. The job will be easier to do without it, although the construction is certainly no big deal. The same design feature can be used with any drywall loft, and the size is variable, depending upon your needs.

Permanent Loft No. 4

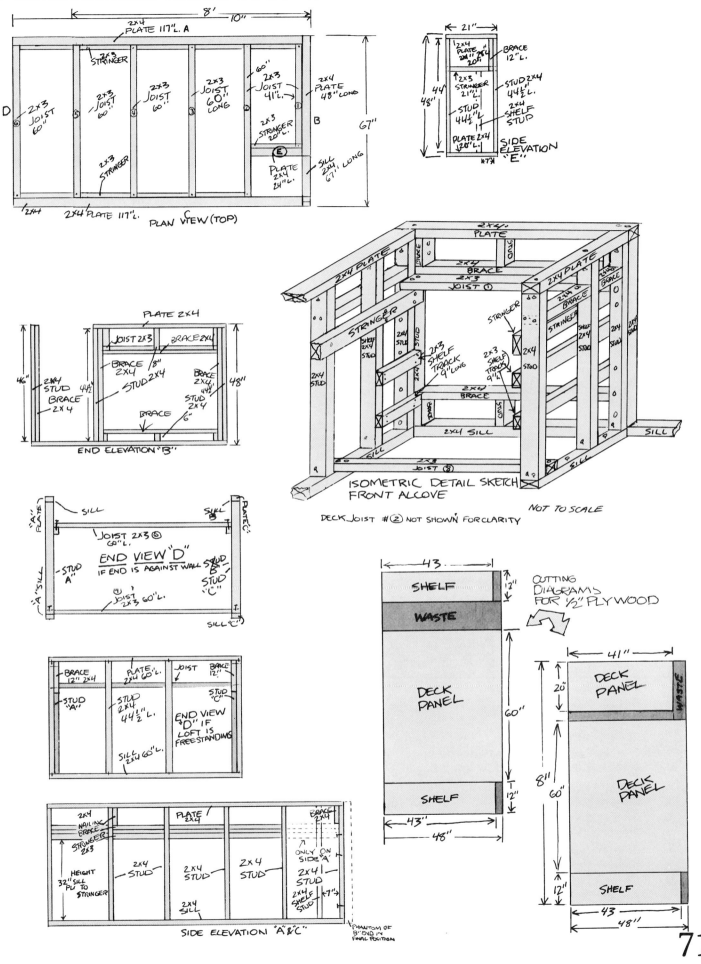

PLAN VIEW (TOP)

SIDE ELEVATION "E"

END ELEVATION "B"

END VIEW "D"
IF END IS AGAINST WALL

ISOMETRIC DETAIL SKETCH
FRONT ALCOVE

DECK JOIST #2 NOT SHOWN FOR CLARITY

NOT TO SCALE

END VIEW "D" IF
LOFT IS FREESTANDING

CUTTING DIAGRAMS
FOR 1/2" PLYWOOD

SHELF

WASTE

DECK PANEL

SHELF

DECK PANEL

WASTE

DECK PANEL

SHELF

SIDE ELEVATION "A & C"

71

LOFT MATTRESSES

A normal box spring and mattress is not the best combination for use in a loft. The price is expensive and the thickness can take away from headroom.

My favorite loft mattress is a urethane foam slab. In most cities, there are stores that specialize in foam rubber, or carry it as a sideline. It comes in every standard mattress size. The price is usually one fourth the cost of a normal type of mattress. A 3″ thick queen-size slab will cost about $30.00. 3/ provides a nice firm slab that is really good for your back. If you like a soft mattress, go to a 4 or 5 inch thickness. It will not cost much more.

A waterbed is not a very good idea for a loft, unless you build a very heavy-duty platform. A good-sized waterbed when filled weighs about a ton.

I've been seeing ads for something called Inflate-a-bed (see below). I haven't been curious enough about it to spend $79.95, but it may be as good as the distributor claims. It's still twice as thick and twice as expensive as urethane foam.

LADDERS

EASY WAY
TO BUILD
A LADDER

CUT AFTER MARKING IF YOU DON'T WANT END TO STICK UP.

DECK

14"

14" THIS IS A GOOD RUNG DISTANCE

14"

2×4 TEMPLATE

2×4 TEMPLATE

CUT AFTER MARKING

QUARTER ROUND OR ANGLE BRACKET

FLOOR

POST

—PROP LADDER RAIL (2×4 OR 2×6). AGAINST DECK, THEN MARK IT USING 2×4 AS GUIDE.

THIS GIVES PROPER ANGLE TO RAIL, IT SITS FLAT ON THE FLOOR—NOT ON THE POINT. TOP CUT IS OPTIONAL.

AFTER CUTTING 2×4 OR 2×6 RUNGS TO WIDTH, NAIL THROUGH RAIL INTO END CENTER OF EACH SIDE ① OF EACH RUNG. WITH LADDER IN WORKING POSITION, ROTATE RUNGS TILL PARALELL TO FLOOR. MARK INSIDE RAIL TO FIX ANGLE, THEN PUT IN MORE NAILS ②

NAIL AT TOP TO ANCHOR

DECK

AFTER FINISHING, PUT A LONG NAIL INTO FLOOR

ANGLE BRACKET

ANGLE BRACKET HOLDS RUNG TO RAIL. NAILS ARE ONLY TO KEEP RUNG FROM ROTATING. ONE BRACKET FOR EACH SIDE OF EACH RUNG. USE SCREWS.

EASIER WAY: BUT NOT AS COMFORTABLE ON BARE FEET.

2×3 LAID FLAT→ ←2×4

NICE VARIATION: DRILL MATCHING HOLES THRU RAIL TO FIT 1" DOWEL. GLUE DOWELS USE NAIL TO SET

←2×4

PLYWOOD LADDER

1×3 TREAD

←2×4
1" QUARTER ROUND MOLDING
←2×3 OR 2×4 BRACE

½" PLYWOOD

Chapter 6

LOFT WIRING

If you intend to have electrical appliances in your loft, you will have to plan for the necessary wiring. By following the procedures on this page you will find that it is a much simpler job than you may have imagined.

First, make a list of the number of outlets your loft will require. Installing outlets in lofts is so simple that it's foolish to use octopus plugs and extension cords. You will probably discover that a double outlet at the head of the loft and two of them at the foot will be sufficient for your needs. Electrical outlets and switches must be mounted in wall boxes. These boxes may be flush or surface mounted. I would recommend mounting them flush with the deck

surface; though in the case of a drywall permanent loft, flush mounting them in the wall may be easier. The best type of wall box to get is the one that is held together by screws.

Measure the amount of cable needed for the job. You will need enough to reach from the nearest wall outlet to your first outlet box, then to any other outlet and to the lighting switch or dimmer, and from there to your lighting. The last step only applies to built-in lighting. Detached lighting should use a normal power cord with plug. In this case, the cable from the switch box should terminate in an outlet box. The cable to use is referred to in the trade as "Romex", and is shown in the detail box.

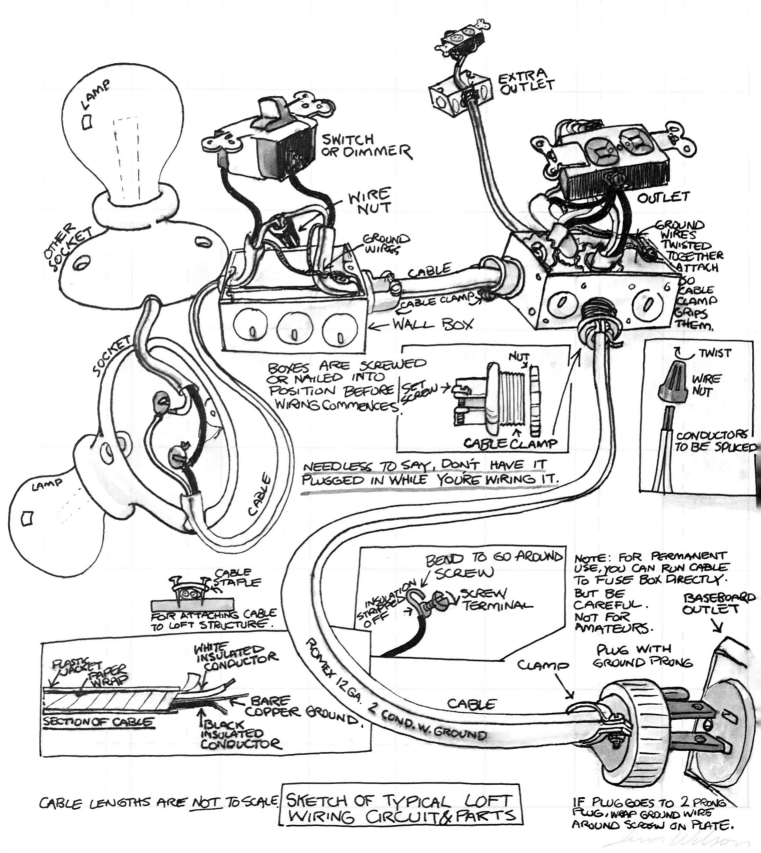

LOFT LIGHTING Chapter 7

Tri-color loft light
in operation:

1. All colors on full. Red overpowers other colors. White is achieved when red is reduced slightly.

2. Green high, Blue medium, Red low.

3. Green low, Blue high, Red medium.

4. Red high, Blue medium, Green low.

Photos by the author.

75

Loft Lighting

The first thing to understand about loft lighting is that it has totally unique problems that can be solved by very few conventional lighting methods. Approaching it as you would a normal room is impossible.

For instance: most rooms use a ceiling fixture for their primary illumination source. In a loft with a 4-or 5 foot ceiling you would be continually bashing the fixture with your head. Or, even if it were in a corner, you would be subject to a great deal of glare. Try standing on a table so that your head is about a foot or two from the ceiling and look at a lighted fixture. You'll have a good idea of how it will work in a loft.

An ordinary table lamp works fine, except in a loft. With its bulky shade, it will consume almost two cubic feet of precious near-floor space. The glare problem with this type of lamp is even worse. Put a table lamp on the floor and sit next to it. You'll notice that if you look in its direction; you're looking over the lampshade directly at the bulb!

Pin-up lamps use a minimal amount of space, but they are plagued by the same glare problems common to the previous methods.

The loft, with its cozy confinement, can be a torture chamber with glaring lights.

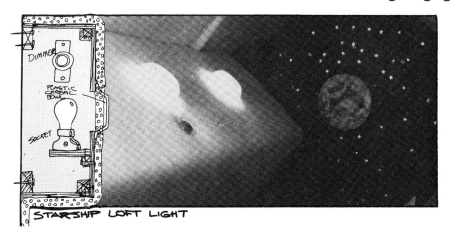
STARSHIP LOFT LIGHT

In the starship loft, since I had to incorporate a big box to conceal a drainpipe anyway, I used three diffused incandescent lights on a common dimmer (see photo). The diffusers were obtained from a five-and-dime store, where they were sold as white plastic cereal bowls. This type of treatment only works if the lamps are within a roomy enclosure. Heat buildup in a confined space would be likely to melt the diffusers. It could also start a fire.

It was very nice lighting, though. Using multiple lamps with dimmers allows for good, even illumination without having one source producing all the light. With the dimmer, three lamps can be used to produce the same amount of light as one normal light. The difference is that the individual lamps only produce 1/3 of the brightness.

The lighting I recommend most highly is indirect with dimmer. There are several reasons for this preference. First, it is almost totally glare-free, as it gently washes the ceiling with light. The effect, especially with a dimmer, is that of soft sunlight. It will almost seem as if the air itself is glowing. The space taken up by an indirect unit, while considerable, is near the ceiling, and usually at the edge of the loft. This is an area that is not nearly so critical as near-floor space.

LOFT LIGHTING

Finally, as you may have gathered from the previous description, indirect is possibly the most sensual lighting imaginable. Candlelight, in comparison, is as harsh as a welder's torch.

The lighting I designed for the Winooski Raftworks loft uses four 60 watt lamps with a dimmer. The lamps are mounted in the cheapest porcelain sockets (39¢) I could find. Since the fixtures cannot normally be seen, appearance is of no importance at all.

THE TRICOLOR LOFT LIGHT

For my third loft, I designed what may possibly be the most sophisticated home lighting device ever. In addition to the good characteristics of variable-brightness indirect lighting, it provides infinitely variable color as well. The tricolor light utilizes the principles of additive color. White light is made up of every color in the spectrum. This is exactly opposite to subtractive color, in which all colors of paint mixed together would produce black.

This unit uses 3 lamps, red, green and blue; each lamp has its own dimmer. You may have noticed that color television uses the same colors to depict any color, or white. The dimmers allow you to mix colored light of any hue or intensity.

To achieve pure color or pure white, the quality of filtration is especially vital. Fortunately, dichroic filtration has been developed recently making it relatively simple to produce very rich pure colored light. A dichroic filter is simply high-temperature transparent colored glass. Previously this quality light could only be achieved by the gel filters commonly used with theatrical lights. Gels are easily melted by heat, so they must be separated from the light source itself, to allow air flow for cooling. This makes for very awkward, bulky lighting.

A dichroic filter can be incorporated into the shell of the lamp itself and still give superior color saturation. The best photo enlargers for color printing use dichroics almost exclusively. Sylvania is now marketing 150-watt dichroic floodlight lamps called "stained-glass floodlights." They are available at almost any lighting supply outlet for under $4.00 and are integral to the tricolor loft light. No other type of colored light bulb will work nearly so well. Amazingly, the cost of lamps, dimmers, sockets and wire is only 25.00. If you already have enough scrap plywood on hand, that will be the entire cost of the light. It has to be one of the greatest bargains around. Construction of this unit is so simple that it can be built in just a few hours with minimal tools. With the dimmers, the dichroic lamps could possibly last forever. I've had mine for over two years and there's not yet the slightest hint of failure.

Although either of the indirect lighting methods can supply adequate light levels for reading, I would recommend augmenting them with wall-mounted high intensity reading lamps. This allows you to maintain a pleasant level of ambient illumination while having concentrated light where you need it. You will find it especially nice if someone wants to sleep while someone else wants to read.

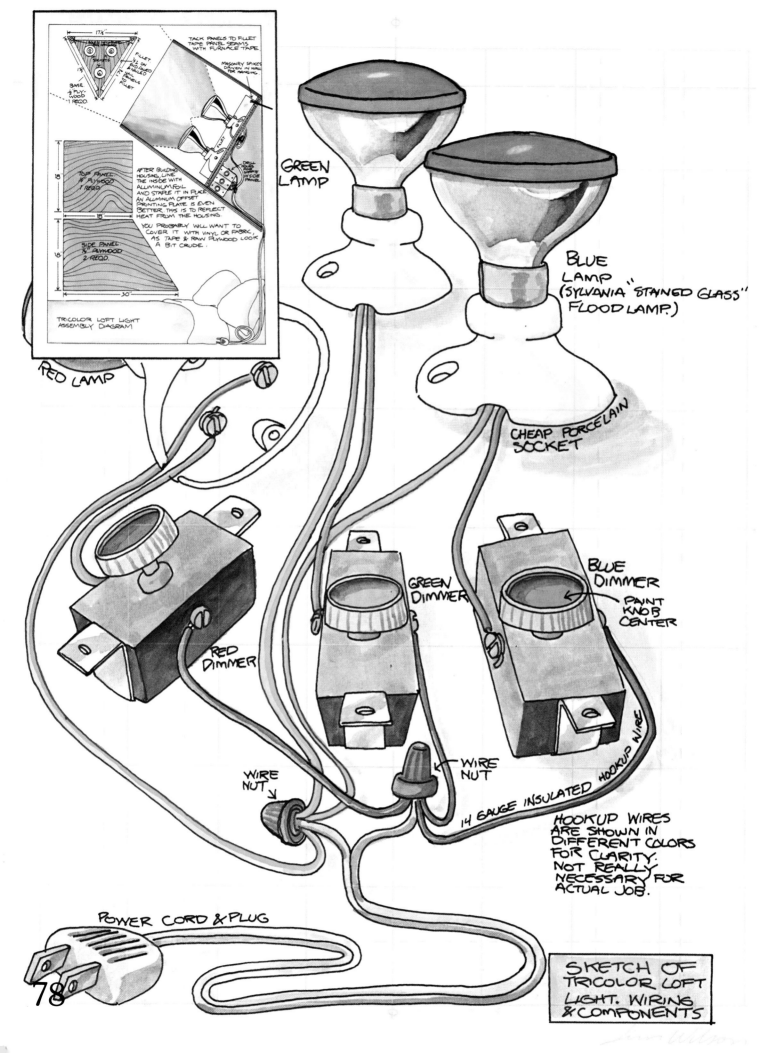

GREEN LAMP

BLUE LAMP ("SYLVANIA "STAINED GLASS" FLOOD LAMP.)

RED LAMP

CHEAP PORCELAIN SOCKET

RED DIMMER

GREEN DIMMER

BLUE DIMMER

PAINT KNOB CENTER

WIRE NUT

WIRE NUT

14 GAUGE INSULATED HOOKUP WIRE

HOOKUP WIRES ARE SHOWN IN DIFFERENT COLORS FOR CLARITY. NOT REALLY NECESSARY FOR ACTUAL JOB.

POWER CORD & PLUG

SKETCH OF TRICOLOR LOFT LIGHT. WIRING & COMPONENTS

Assembly Diagram inset:

TACK PANELS TO FILLET TAPE PANEL SEAMS WITH FURNACE TAPE

MASONRY SPIKES DRIVEN IN WALL FOR HANGING

FILLET ½ ON END GLUED & NAILED NAIL PANELS TO FILLET

BASE ⅜ PLYWOOD 1 REQD.

17½

TOP PANEL ¾ PLYWOOD 1 REQD.

18

18

SIDE PANEL ¾ PLYWOOD 2 REQD.

18

30

DRILL HOLES FOR SHAFTS IN SIDE PANEL

AFTER BUILDING HOUSING, LINE THE INSIDE WITH ALUMINUM FOIL AND STAPLE IT IN PLACE. AN ALUMINUM OFFSET PRINTING PLATE IS EVEN BETTER. THIS IS TO REFLECT HEAT FROM THE HOUSING.

YOU PROBABLY WILL WANT TO COVER IT WITH VINYL OR FABRIC, AS TAPE & RAW PLYWOOD LOOK A BIT CRUDE.

TRICOLOR LOFT LIGHT ASSEMBLY DIAGRAM

Commercial Loftbuilders

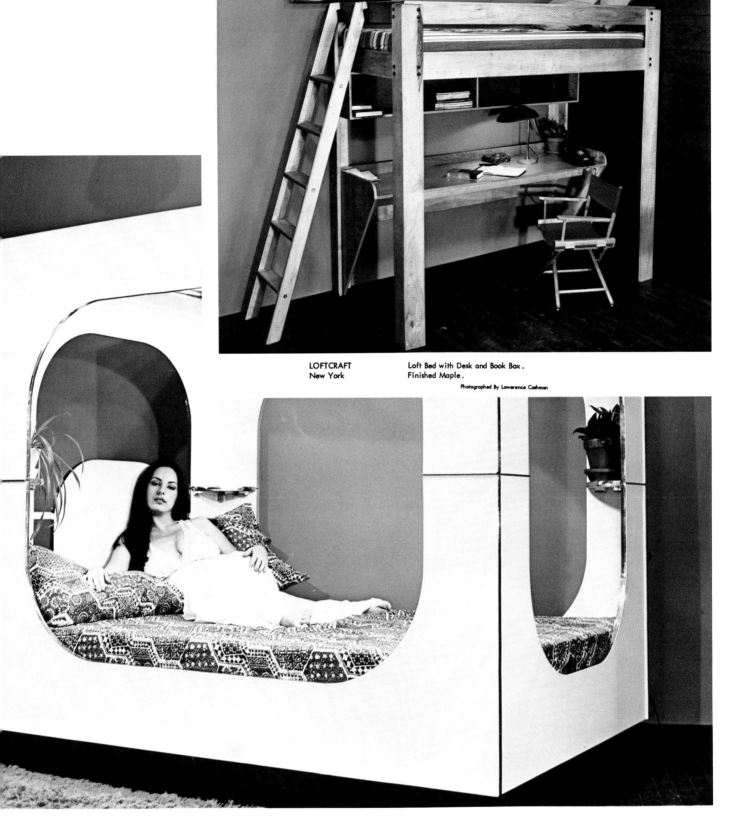

LOFTCRAFT
New York

Loft Bed with Desk and Book Box.
Finished Maple.

Photographed By Lawerence Cashman

LOFTCRAFT
New York

The Sleep Box with Mirrored Ceiling.
Also Available in Walnut & Oak.

Photographed By Lawerence Cashman

Chapter 8
COMMERCIAL LOFTBUILDERS

If for some reason you don't want to build your own loft, there is still hope. In most large cities, there are people who will gladly do the job for you.

There are two basic types of commercial lofts, prefabricated, and those built on location. From what I have seen so far, the prefabs are invariably of BTL Design. The built-on-location lofts can be either BTL or permanent designs.

Your best bet may be in looking through the classified section of your local newspaper under carpentry or interior design and renovation. If you live in N.Y.C., all you have to do is leaf through the VILLAGE VOICE, and you'll find at least a dozen loft builders.

The color photos opening this chapter are by LOFTCRAFT, probably the King of the Commercial Loft Builders, Furniture Division. The top photo is of the PARSONS loft. It isn't called that because it looks like a parsons table, but because its designer and President of the company is Randy Parsons. It's a clean, efficient design in maple. There are lots of modular accessories you can add; shelves, tables, couches, closets, etc. They disassemble easily (carriage bolts) and I'm sure they can be shipped anywhere.

The other color photo is of their sleep box, which I consider a loft, even if they don't. All the panels are hinged for compact traveling. The corner shelves keep every thing locked together and rigid. I think it's a really clever design, although it may be a bit too spacey-slick for some people.

You can get more information from:

LOFTCRAFT
120 West 20th St.
New York, N.Y. 10011
(212) 255-9048

Also in New York:

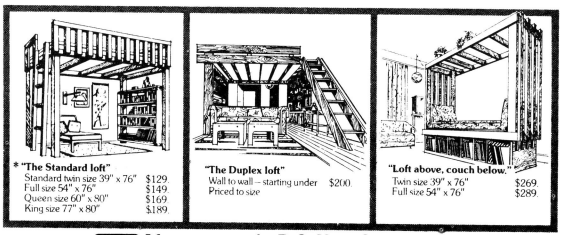

* **"The Standard loft"**
Standard twin size 39" x 76" $129.
Full size 54" x 76" $149.
Queen size 60" x 80" $169.
King size 77" x 80" $189.

"The Duplex loft"
Wall to wall – starting under $200.
Priced to size

"Loft above, couch below."
Twin size 39" x 76" $269.
Full size 54" x 76" $289.

I don't have much information about these people, because I was never able to reach them on the phone. Maybe you'll have better luck.

in Philadelphia:

John Meade

John Meade, who did the vinyl-sculptured loft on page 17, custom-designs only, no prefabs, no mail orders. I'm sure he'd be glad to jump on a plane, though. It would be pretty expensive, but he does an amazing loft.

John Meade
312 S. Camac St.
Philadelphia, Pa. 19172
(215) KI 5-6487

Carpenter Carl Beason

Carl Beason, who did the construction on the Elizabethan Loft is also known as "The Singing Carpenter". He's based in Philadelphia, and can build anything, especially lofts. He's probably typical of good freelance carpenters all over the continent. It may take a bit of looking, but you can find one near you.

Carpenter Carl Beason
(215) 755-1264

Chapter 9
Loft Audio Systems

After setting up my first loft I made a startling discovery — namely that the music system I had been using sounded three times as good in the loft as it had in my living room. The fact that the loft was sound proofed had a lot to do with the different quality. But as I found out later, more conventional lofts with a minimum of acoustic designing also delivered improved fidelity.

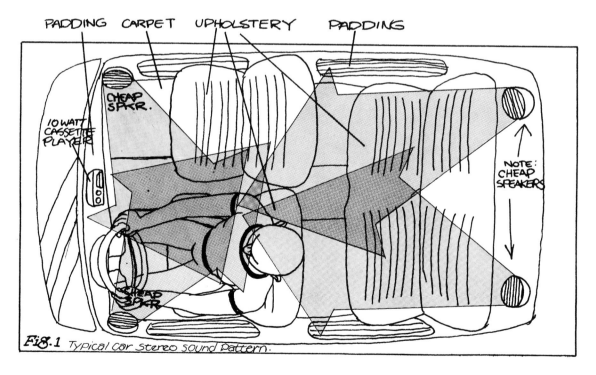

Fig. 1 Typical car stereo sound pattern.

I'm sure that you've experienced car stereo before, and if you know anything about audio equipment, you will have noted that most car stereo units have approximately 10 watts of power per channel with a

LOFT SOUND

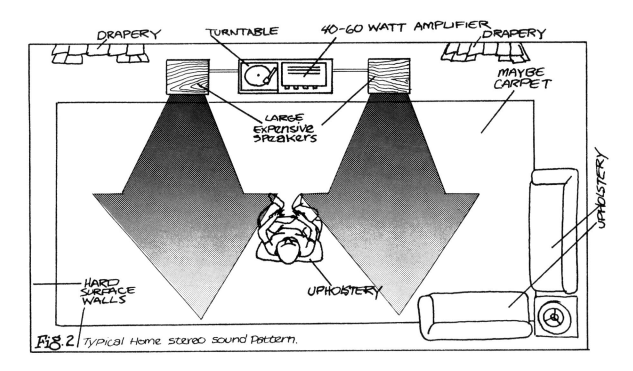

DRAPERY   TURNTABLE   40-60 WATT AMPLIFIER   DRAPERY

MAYBE CARPET

LARGE EXPENSIVE SPEAKERS

UPHOLSTERY

HARD SURFACE WALLS   UPHOLSTERY

Fig.2 Typical Home stereo sound Pattern.

few 5″ low-fi speakers in ridiculously minimal enclosures. Contrasted with the usual home unit of 25-50 watts per channel fed into acoustic suspension speakers in sophisticated enclosures, the car unit is almost laughable. Yet in a car environment, the minimal system will deliver terrific sound.

Consider the car as an acoustic space. It's small, mostly enclosed, and has lots of upholstery and padding. Also, the speakers are usually located so that the listener is sitting within the sound pattern. One does not need to be an audio engineer to notice the similarity between the loft and the car. If you've gone

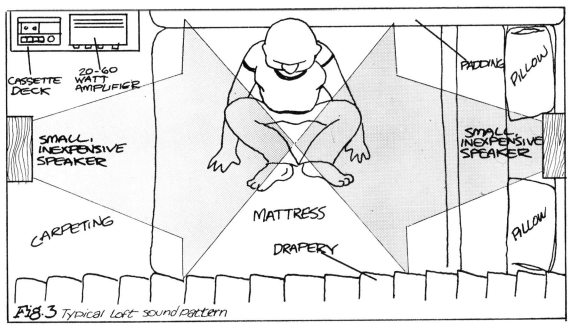

CASSETTE DECK   20-60 WATT AMPLIFIER

PADDING   PILLOW

SMALL, INEXPENSIVE SPEAKER   SMALL, INEXPENSIVE SPEAKER

CARPETING   MATTRESS   PILLOW

DRAPERY

Fig.3 Typical Loft sound pattern

LOFT SOUND

shopping for audio gear at a quality sound store you've probably also noted that the listening room is small, enclosed, padded and carpeted. If you've bought a system tested in such a space, it's likely that it didn't sound quite as impressive when you got it home. Now you know why.

There are other similarities between the car and loft other than acoustic properties. Chief among them is small physical space requirements needed for components. If you think back about 10 years, you will recall that several equipment manufacturers offered record players for car installation. Then came the tape cassette and cartridges, nowadays the only place you can find a car record player is the goodwill store. The reason is simple. Tape and the playback machine occupy much less space than a turntable and records, and are much less prone to vibration hassles.

I would definitely recommend tape cassettes over cartridges and either of them over a turntable in a loft. However if you have the extra space for record storage, and have an extra turntable, go ahead and use it.

You will have to put it on a surface that's not a mechanical part of the loft. Most lofts, especially the deck, are rather flexible. Therefore every time you move around, the tone arm will skip, unless of course, the turntable is sitting on a shelf attached to a wall of the room. Notice that I said 'of the room'. A loft wall is just as prone to vibration and sway as the deck because force applied to the deck is transmitted to every part of the loft and those surfaces connected to it.

The biggest difference between a car tape deck and one for the home is that the home unit uses household current (115 VAC). Many car units offer a converter for use of the unit on 115 VAC. You can also make your own rather easily (SEE SCHEMATIC).

My personal recommendation would be a combination of a 20 watt receiver (amplifier and stereo tuner in the same cabinet) combined with a stereo cassette deck. The receiver should cost about 75.00 maximum and the deck about the same. You should be able to find a used receiver rather easily, since this type is commonly bought and then traded in rather quickly because it really doesn't have enough power for a normal sized room. Don't buy a used cassette deck, most people don't get rid of them unless the deck is worn or defective.

Concerning speakers:

Although you can use the little speakers that screw onto car door panels I wouldn't advise it unless you really want to build a cheap system. For a little more money, you can do much better. If you have a bolt-together or open loft, you should get bookshelf-type speakers and enclosures for mounting on a wall or shelf. They can also be screwed to the railing. My current Radio Shack sale catalog has a 6 1/2 x 15 3/4 x 7 1/2 bookshelf speaker shown for 14.95, that would probably work very nicely. If you're building a drywall loft, you can build a speaker into the wall very simply and get good sound with less space at a lower cost.

I've included a little ad for speaker hangers. The hangers allow you to suspend speakers outside of an open loft to save space.

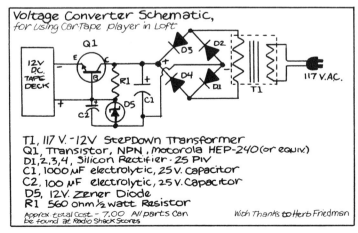

Voltage Converter Schematic,
for using Car Tape player in Loft

T1, 117 V. - 12V Stepdown Transformer
Q1, Transistor, NPN, Motorola HEP-240 (or equiv.)
D1,2,3,4, Silicon Rectifier - 25 PIV
C1, 1000 µF electrolytic, 25 V. Capacitor
C2, 100 µF electrolytic, 25 V. Capacitor
D5, 12V. Zener Diode
R1 560 ohm ½ watt Resistor
Approx. total cost - 7.00 All parts can be found at Radio Shack Stores
With Thanks to Herb Friedman

LOFT SOUND

Loft Speaker PROCEDURE

Before studs are sheathed with gypsum board, cut 2x3 barriers and baffles. Barriers should have tight friction fit. After drilling holes, nail & glue baffles between barriers 2 & 3; then glue & nail barriers in place between studs.
2-conductor speaker wire is run from plenum thru 1" hole in barrier #2, then thru ¼" hole in barrier #3 then down to floor. After this, studs are sheathed & plywood front panel can be cut & speaker mounted to it.
Panel may be painted or cloth covered to protect speaker cone.

After connecting speaker to leads, panel is screwed down tightly. Bottom lead is then connected to amplifier. You will be amazed by the sound quality of this design, especially bass.

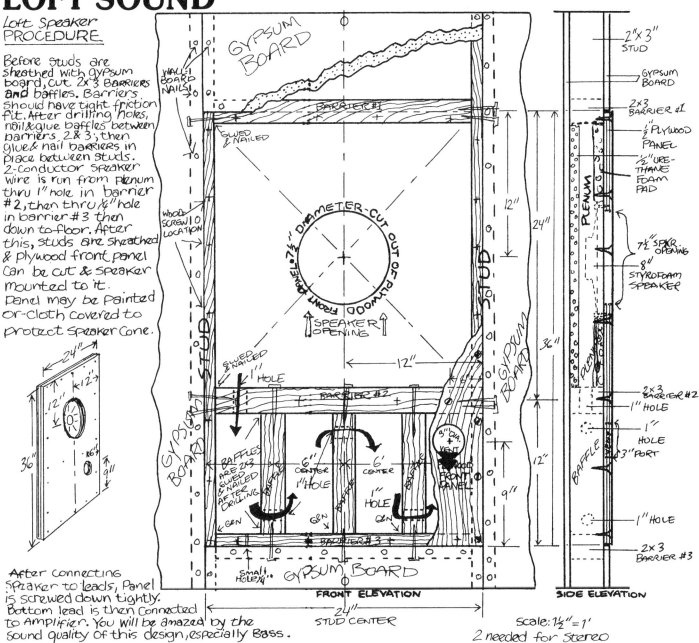

GYPSUM BOARD
WALL BOARD NAILS
BARRIER #1
GLUED & NAILED
WOOD SCREW LOCATION
.75 DIAMETER - CUT OUT OF PLYWOOD FRONT PANEL
SPEAKER OPENING
STUD
GLUED & NAILED
1" HOLE
BARRIER #2
BAFFLES ARE 2x3 GLUED & NAILED AFTER DRILLING
BAFFLE
6" CENTER
1" HOLE
6" CENTER
1" HOLE
BAFFLE
3" DIA. VENT
WOOD FRONT PANEL
G&N
BARRIER #3
GYPSUM BOARD
SMALL HOLE ¼"
GYPSUM BOARD
12"
24"
36"
12"
9"
FRONT ELEVATION
24"
STUD CENTER

SIDE ELEVATION
2" x 3" STUD
GYPSUM BOARD
2x3 BARRIER #1
½" PLYWOOD PANEL
½" URETHANE FOAM PAD
PLENUM
7½" SPKR OPENING
8" STYROFOAM SPEAKER
2x3 BARRIER #2
1" HOLE
1" HOLE
3" PORT
BAFFLE
1" HOLE
2x3 BARRIER #3

Scale: 1½" = 1'
2 needed for stereo

24"
12"
12"
36"
6"
9"

CAT. NO. 42-1343
SPECIFICATIONS

Power capability: 20 watts peak
Frequency range: 40 Hz — 20 kHz
Sensitivity: 90 dB/M for 1 watt electrical input
Input impedance: 8 ohms
Operating temperature range: $-20°F$ to $+175°F$
Size: Round 8" diameter, 1" depth
Weight: 11 oz.

FREQUENCY RESPONSE

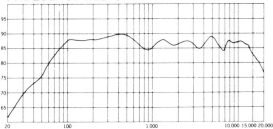

Revolutionary New Concept in Ultra-Thin Loud Speaker Designs.

This speaker is plastic-framed with a styrofoam cone. The catalog No. is Radio Shack's, but I've gotten them at Lafayette Radio stores also. Price is about 12.00 each.

LOFT SOUND

THE FOLLOWING IS AN UNPAID TESTIMONIAL

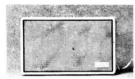
I'm positive that the president of Advent Corporation sleeps in a loft. There can be no other reason for an outfit whose most well-known product costs $4000.00 (the Advent 84 inch wall television) to design and market a speaker like the one in the ad below.

When the fact is added that Advent also makes one of the few professional-quality cassette decks, my conslusion is almost inescapable.

Mr. Advent is putting the finishing touches on his new loft. He had already marketed the Advent cassette deck with Dolby, probably one of the first commercial applications for the Dolby noise suppression circuit. I think he designed the Deck before Dolby designed the circuit, and was just waiting for a tape breakthrough. Mr. Advent is that kind of guy, a visionary you might say.

Anyway, Mr. Advent has just installed his Dolby cassette deck and a stereo receiver that he doesn't want to market until the price of the computerized tuning circuit on it can be built for $200.00. He has just wrestled a pair of Advent loudspeakers up the ladder into the loft. He suddenly realizes that there's not enough room for them and the refrigerator too.

He designes a miniature hi-fi speaker and has the boys in the shop build them as prototypes.

He puts the speakers in the loft, maybe he even puts four of them in, they're small enough.

A week later, the treasurer of Advent says "What's this about the boys in the shop working 6 hours overtime building 6″ x 11″ speaker prototypes?"

"Are you crazy, who'd want a good speaker that little?" or something like that. Mr. Advent would reply,

"Oh those, they're for a little super quality FM table radio we're working on."

The treasurer says "That sounds like something that would sell," and goes on down the hall.

"Whew, guess I'll have to tell the boys in the lab to start work on that radio," breathes Mr. Advent, as he mops his brow.

Later the treasurer suggests that since the FM table radio is such a big seller, maybe they should try to sell those terrific little speakers separately. So they run this ad in **Rolling Stone**.

The story above is fiction, of course. Although there is an Advent Corporation and they make all those products I mentioned. There is no one named Mr. Advent connected with them, I hope. But that does sound like the only explanation, unless Mr. Advent drives a van. If that imaginary computerized receiver comes out as a clock radio, we'll know for sure.

I highly recommend this speaker for lofts. As far as I'm concerned it is the ultimate loft speaker. It's small, cheap and sounds great in a small space. I've included the coupon that ran with the ad and added the boxes for the cassette deck and the TV, so you can find out where to buy them, if you wish.

Chapter 10
Loft Phone Installation

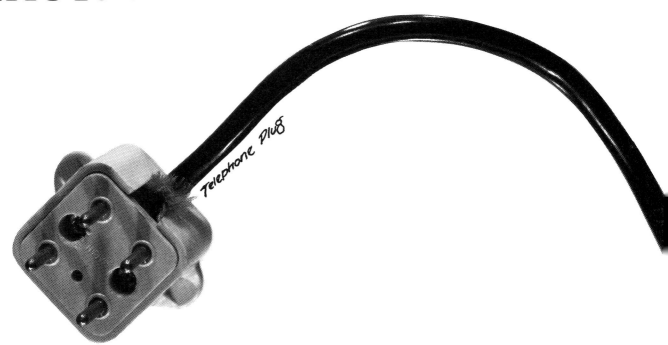

Telephone Plug

I strongly recommend that you have an extension telephone in your loft. There is nothing more frustrating than hearing the telephone ring and having to scramble down a ladder, risking life and limb, only to reach it too late. Going through the same process in darkness can be fatal. There is no reason at all to avoid having a loft phone.

The simplest way of solving the problem, of course, is to call the phone company and have them do the job. Installation will cost about 12.00, with a couple of bucks a month rental for the phone itself. This is also the only legal way to do it.

The not-as-simple-but-much-cheaper way is to install your own extension phone. The phone company frowns upon this solution; and, if they find out about it they'll tell you to remove it or lose your phone service.

For obvious reasons, I'm not going to advise anyone to violate the telephone tariff regulations. However, I will give complete instructions in this section to satisfy your curiosity.

LOFT PHONE

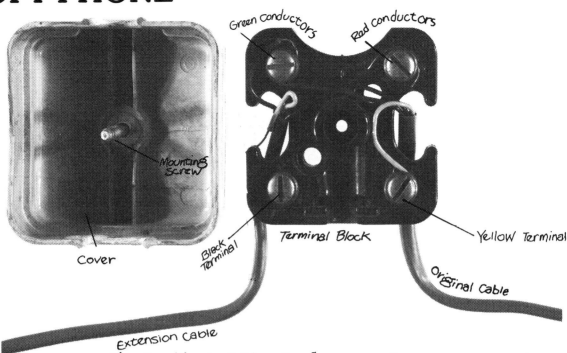

Green conductors
Red conductors
Mounting Screw
Cover
Black Terminal
Terminal Block
Yellow Terminal
Original Cable
Extension cable

Fig. 1, Typical Terminal Box With Cover Removed

If you will notice, your telephone cord leads to a small grey box, usually mounted to a baseboard. There is a screw in the center of the cap. If this screw is loosened, the cap will come off. Under it is a base plate with four screw terminals. It will have from 2 to 4 color coded wires coming out of the system cable to the screws. The leads from your phone cord also go to these screws. On most phone sets, only 2 wires are actually used, red and green. For your purposes the other 2 screws can be ignored.

If your home has jacks installed already, you won't need to bother with the foregoing information.

You will need enough hookup wire to extend from the baseboard box to your loft deck, preferably following the baseboard to avoid wire clutter. The best hookup wire to use is the real telephone company item. You may even have some around that the installer left when he installed your phone. If you don't have any, 2 or 3 conductor thermostat hookup wire will do nicely. Conductors are the small colored wires inside the grey cable. Thermostat wire is also color coded. The different colors enable you to hook the phone up easily and properly.

The red and green wires of the cable are connected to the screw terminals with those same colored wires from the phone system attached. The other ends of the cable's red and green wires are hooked up to the terminals of a telephone jack. Both thermostat wire and telephone jacks may be purchased at a wide variety of electronic supply sources. If the telephone you're installing doesn't have a plug on its cord, you can buy the plug there also. The terminals of the plug are attached to their corresponding color code. The terminals are always marked R (red), G (green), B (black), and Y (yellow). It's probably best to hook up the jack and plug before mounting and hooking up the baseboard end to the terminal box. If you don't have an extra phone, you can buy one at almost any electronic supply house. I find that a wall phone is best in a loft.

If your loft is in a different room from your present telephone, it probably isn't worth the trouble of doing the job yourself. Especially since you'll have to disconnect everything if a phone repairman is needed in the future.

The phone company makes a fantastic profit on extension phones, so they are not going to give up their monopoly without a fight. There is an ongoing program involved with checking people's lines to find unauthorized extensions. Actually the phone company's tests only show how many bells are on the circuit; thus many people disconnect the bell to avoid being caught.

Chapter 11

FLOOR COVERING

Unless you are really crazy about hardwood floors, the only floor covering I would recommend is carpeting. It provides a warmer ambience to the space, better acoustic properties, and your mattress won't be as likely to slide around. You could use Astro Turf, but it is really soft in appearance only.

Most lofts have deck areas of a size that permits using a carpet remnant — saving lots of money. You don't even need to find a piece that is the same width as your deck. Since the mattress covers most of the deck anyway, you can easily piece the carpet so that most of the seam is concealed by the mattress.

When I carpet a loft, I usually install the carpet wall-to-wall, tacking it around the edges and along any seams. To really finish it off, lay 3/4" quarter-round molding where the wall meets the carpet, mitering at corners. Carpet scraps can be used to cover your ladder treads; glue them on with contact cement.

WALL COVERING

You can't go too wrong with paint; but you can also cover your walls with cloth, vinyl, foam rubber, acoustic tile, or carpet. The important thing is that you like it. The loft will be much more cheerful if you use a light color, however. The more soft, sound absorbing surfaces there are in the loft, especially on the walls, the better the acoustics will be.

The walls and ceiling of my starship loft were covered by 1" thick urethane foam that came on a roll. It worked so well that the sounds of a hundred dressmakers coming to work at 7 a.m. in the factory above didn't wake me. And my stereo sounded great, too. Foam for a 5 x 10 x 4 loft cost about $30.00. I glued it to surfaces with contact cement. Finger foam would really be great for a loft, since it looks so interesting.

I once saw some Astro Turf in a carpet store that was rainbow striped. I thought at the time that it would be nice for loft walls, but I haven't run into any recently.

If you want soft walls for acoustic purposes; but want a painted wall surface, just glue a carpet panel to the painted wall — anything helps.

Chapter 12
Suppliers

Edmund Scientific Co.

The Edmund Scientific catalog has thousands of hard-to-get and frequently unheard of items. I have used them for years, and they are often the only source for certain exotic items — mostly of an optical nature. A large portion of their catalog is devoted to light show items. Many of these are really hokey but there is enough basic stuff to make the catalog well worth ordering. Probably the only mail order source for dichroic floodlights and projection lenses.

Catalog from:

Edmund Scientific Co.
100 Edscorp Bldg.
Barrington, N.J. 08007

Herbach & Rademann

H & R has a terrific monthly catalog of surplus electrical and electronic equipment. They are a good source for air blowers, fans, and cheap videotape equipment. In general you will find lower prices than Edmunds on a lot of items.

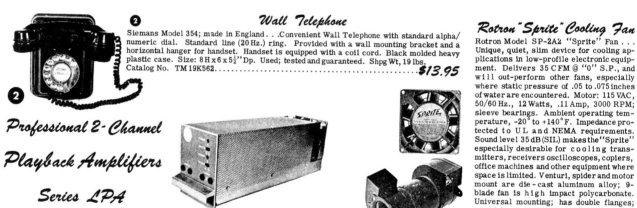

❷ **Wall Telephone**

Siemens Model 354; made in England. . .Convenient Wall Telephone with standard alpha/numeric dial. Standard line (20 Hz.) ring. Provided with a wall mounting bracket and a horizontal hanger for handset. Handset is equipped with a coil cord. Black molded heavy plastic case. Size: 8 H x 6 x 5½''Dp. Used; tested and guaranteed. Shpg Wt, 19 lbs. Catalog No. TM 19K562 . . . . **$13.95**

Professional 2-Channel
Playback Amplifiers
Series LPA

Type LPA102A MI-371035A. . . Standard Two-Channel Amplifier, as described.
Catalog No. TM 18K859 . . . . **$20.00**

Rotron "Sprite" Cooling Fan
Rotron Model SP-2A2 "Sprite" Fan . . . Unique, quiet, slim device for cooling applications in low-profile electronic equipment. Delivers 35 CFM @ "0" S.P., and will out-perform other fans, especially where static pressure of .05 to .075 inches of water are encountered. Motor: 115 VAC, 50/60 Hz., 12 Watts, .11 Amp, 3000 RPM; sleeve bearings. Ambient operating temperature, -20° to +140°F. Impedance protected to UL and NEMA requirements. Sound level 35 dB (SIL) makes the "Sprite" especially desirable for cooling transmitters, receivers oscilloscopes, copiers, office machines and other equipment where space is limited. Venturi, spider and motor mount are die-cast aluminum alloy; 9-blade fan is high impact polycarbonate. Universal mounting; has double flanges; mount in any position. Air flow is reversible by turning fan end-for-end. Size: 3⅛ x 3¼ x 1⅝'' deep; fits standard 3½'' high EIA racks. Terminals can be soldered, or use a Rotron #30787 plug (not supplied). Dull black finish. New. Shpg Wt, 2 lbs.
Cat. No. TM 19K857 . . . . **$8.00**

Monthly catalog from: **Herbach & Rademan, Inc.**
401 East Erie Ave.
Philadelphia, Pa. 19134

Fasco Dual Blower

Silvo Hardware

Silvo sells top quality tools and hardware. In addition to consumer-grade equipment, they carry heavy-duty professional tools and accessories. They ship anywhere.

No. 4100 Rockwell Single Speed ⅜" drill— Double insulated to protect the user. Ball thrust bearing construction. Double reduction gears. 3-jaw geared chuck. UL Listed. Includes chuck key and holder.
1000 RPM—2.7 amps—
4100-R7 P—4 lbs. . . . . . . (APL) Tool—$10.99
4100-R7 . . . . (APL)—.$9.35

Catalog from:
Silvo Hardware Co.
107-109 Walnut St.
Philadelphia, Pa. 19106

Poly Paks

I've been ordering things from Poly-Paks since I was building crystal radios in the fifties. I've always been pleased by their low prices, good merchandise and fast service. After you order something, they send you a little catalog at least once a month, full of their latest offerings and their usual merchandise: transistors, computer circuits and other electronic bargain items. Write for Catalog from:

Has the following controls on front panel, PHONO-STEREO-AM-FM, MONO, FM STEREO, GUITAR, TAPE, MIKE master control switch. LOUDNESS, BALANCE, TREBLE, BASS controls, with power ON-OFF rocker switch, and AFC ON-OFF. Designed for all audio-philes to use as wall unit in DEN or FAMILY ROOM, or control unit by easy chair in family room, or for those who wish to design their own console or modular system. With 6 ft. 115 VAC cord and plug. Only 13 x 7 x 3½" deep. Features: 4-speaker system, built-in FM antenna, record player jacks on separate panel. Another external panel consists of provisions for external FM and AM antenna, "satellite" speakers to provide 4-speaker ground, jacks for connecting a tape recorder to radio tuner or phono of systems to record. Lower inputs for connecting tape deck that will play back thru the internal amplifier for systems. AC jack for phono power connection. RED, GREEN and CLEAR indicators for Phono, AM, and FM respectively. Includes red indicator on front panel for STEREO indicator. Has separate input to plug into mike, guitar and other musical instruments. Shpg. wt. 3 lbs. With knobs.

$33.95
Cat. No. 92CU2414
LESS ESCUTCHEON

SLIM-LINE WALL OR CABINET
AM-FM-MULTIPLEX
"CONSOLE POWER*"
SOLID STATE TUNER AMPLIFIER!
Same unit used to power expensive U.S. made console stereos!

Diamond style cartridge!
16-33-45-78 rpm!

$19.95
4-SPEED RECORD CHANGER

Economy, inflation-fighting priced full-size record changer. (13x11"). It's loaded with features: . . . light weight tubular tone armful fidelity ceramic cartridge, low "WOW and RUMBLE" heavy-duty constructed base, easy mechanism places arm on the exact spot on record, positive action slide controls for REJ. ON, OFF, 7", 10", 12" records. Also slide control for 16-33-45-78 rpm speeds. It's a natural for our economy DO-IT-YOURSELF systems. 5 lbs. Individually boxed with hookup instructions. **Cat. No. 92CU2482.**

QUAD
TAPE DECK
Only **$19.95**

JUST IN . . .

The "QUADS". Use for either 8-track or tapes. An audiophile economy exclusive by Poly Paks. Same type found in the most expensive tape players, tuners, etc. It's a complete Quad system, featuring 4-channel preamp . . . all the cables necessary to just plug into any stereo quad amplifier or even our 20 & 60-watt tuner amplifier systems (see elsewhere in this catalog). Insert a cartridge to turn on deck. Enjoy up to 80 minutes of non-stop, non-repeat stereo or quad. Remove cartridge deck automatically shuts off. Other features: 4-program indicator lights, automatic or manual program change, push-button channel selector switch, built-in triggering switch that enables you to automatically use 8-track or quad tapes; heavy-duty flywheel for WOW & FLUTTER PROOF sound; flapping front panel tape door mounting front panel flange.

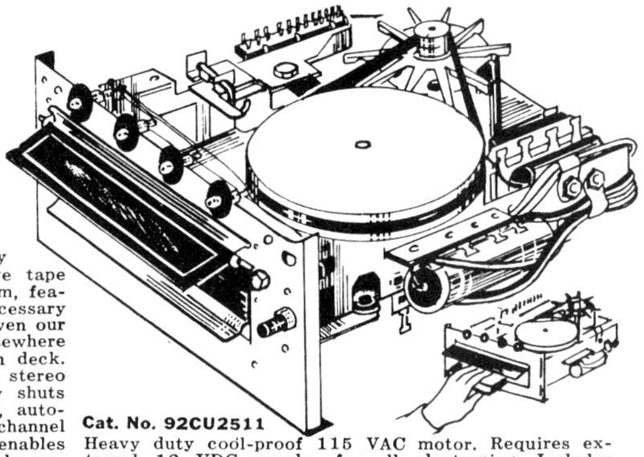

Cat. No. 92CU2511
Heavy duty cool-proof 115 VAC motor. Requires external 12 VDC supply, for all electronics. Includes schematic, hookups, all cables. Size: 6½ x 6½ x 3½". IT'S READY TO GO!

111 MM PROJECTION PRECISION PROJECTION LENS
Worth many times our asking price. Made by one of the leading lens manufacturers in USA. (Sorry, can't mention name). Originally used in $1,000 photo copy machine. Focal length 111 mm (4⅜", speed of aperture F/5.6, image coverage 8½ diagonal, image to object distance 17½". Multi element. Coated lenses). O.D. 1.725. Wt. 8 oz. **Cat. No. 92CU1511**

Only $3.95

Buy 2 for stereo

"2001" BEEPIN' ALARM GIANT DIGIT CLOCK KIT
6-DIGITS
BEEP
B-E-E-P
Only **$39.95**
Character height 0.6"

Giant "NO GLARE" red filtered panel. 10 minute SNOOZE ALARM. The complete SILENCE of the clock gives us the eerie feeling of the Year-2001. Featuring also AM-PM indicators by using two red LED'S that are ON every 12 hours — therefore you control whether the LED'S be AM or PM. 3 push buttons and toggle control hours, minutes, alarms and AM-PM indications. EASY TO BUILD! FUN! Instruction booklet. With rubber mounting on cabinet. Power 115VAC. Size 7¾ x 7 x 2½". Wt. 2 lbs. **Cat. No. 92CU2350.**

IT'S NEW! From the famous KRONOS people at an "alarmin'" low price. Uses famous "MK" Beepin' clock chip. That's right, can you imagine a clock chip that's within itself — B-E-E-P-S! It's the "tomorrow" chip today. Uses the famous all LED MAN-6 or equal readouts from the big "M" people. Minimum parts, in attractive walnut cabinet with black crackle tone.

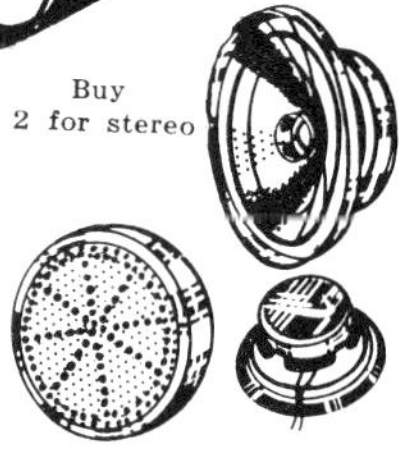

FLUSH MOUNT HIGH POWER
Cloth roll air-suspension cones, hi compliance, 5¼" dia. wide range freq., 13/16" voice coil, 8 ohms, with acoustic cushion snap-on grills for best fidelity sound. Extended high and low end despite size for music and high speech intelligibility.

Cat. No.	Oz. Mag.	Watts	2 for
92CU2201	10	25	$14.00

POWER PAK
$2.95
92CU2336
Nifty 12 VDC 275 mil power supply. 2" square. Excellent for 100's of transistor type projects and calculators too! Plug in 110 VAC — PRESTO instant power supply. COMPACT! With 6 foot cord, plug and jack set. Input 120 VAC 60 hz. Wt. 6 oz.

COMPLETE LIQUID CRYSTAL WRIST WATCH
This is no kit
49.95
gift boxed

Unconditionally guaranteed for one year.

Poly Paks has outdone all jewelry houses, department stores, by giving you this neat 3½ digit complete wrist watch. Same type unit sold elsewhere for as much as $250. An amazing saving. Complete with energy cell. READY TO GO. Sorry we cannot name manufacturer. Made in U.S.A. All MOS ics by Solid State Scientific. Heavy duty GOLD case. Comes with wrist watch band.

☐ Cat. No. 92CU2149 **GOLD**
☐ Cat. No. 92CU2222 **SILVER**

Instructions included

ALLIANCE SHADE POLE BLOWER 115VAC
4.95

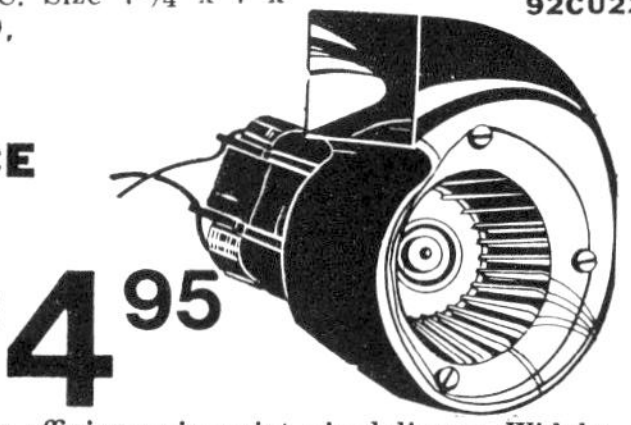

Offers maximum efficiency in quiet air delivery. Widely used in hearing, ventilating, exhausting, cooling equipment. Direct drive motors 100 CFM. Open frame shaded pole motor, driving a Torrington 2½ x 2" bladed wheel, square 2¼ x 2" intake, 2½ x 2" outlet holes. Overall size of housing 5½ x 2½ x 5" deep. Wt. 2 lbs. 3 - 10/32 mtg. holes. **Cat. No. 92CU2507**

BIRD CALL
$4.95
AB-7 

This bird call simulator electronically reproduces the songs of canaries, parakeets and other exotic warbling birds. To operate—needs' only: A small, 8-ohm PM speaker, any 1½-V battery, and SPST switch. Size: 1½ x 1¼ x 1". **Cat. No. 92CU1932**

Poly-Paks, Inc.
P.O. Box 942
South Lynnfield, Mass. 01940

Metropolitan Teletronics

These people sell almost any sort of telephone you can imagine. Prices range from $10.00 to $200.00. They also sell wire, jacks, etc.

TYPE 80/90 EXTENSION PHONES
by Automatic Electric

These phones are the latest style models in a wide variety of decorator colors for use wherever another extension is needed at home or in the office. Sturdily constructed, they contain variable volume ringer, dial, cable and 4-prong plug for easy and trouble-free installation.

8-8090—Colors: Black, White, Beige, Blue, Green, Ivory, Pink, Red, & Yellow $29.95
plus $1.50 shipping charge

ROMAN CANDLE PHONE

A beautiful, hand-crafted vertical column terminated by a continental telephone. It is approximately four feet tall and has a slender silhouette that blends well with either modern or traditional decor. Available in a choice of three finishes. Ready for instant use; comes with dial, ringer, cord and plug.

8-48—Antique Earth Gold ....
8-48A—Antique Kyoto Silver ....
8-48B—Burnished Gold $199.95
plus $3.00 shipping charge

Request catalog from:

**Metropolitan Teletronics
35 West 35th St.
New York, N.Y. 10001**

THRONE BATHROOM PHONE

Be the person to have everything! Here is comfort-plus! No need to step out of the shower when the phone rings. Colors: beige, white, black, gray.
8-ZE32—Bathroom Phone $19.95
8-136R—Ringer box if needed $6.95
plus $1.50 shipping charge

REGULAR PAY STATION PHONE
with dial

This pay station model is an ideal extension unit for use in a variety of places. It can also serve many decorative purposes. No coins are needed for this unit. It comes complete with simple installation instructions, ready for hanging, with dial, ringer, regular receiver, cable and plug.

8-67XF—Black with Silver trim only $79.95
plus $7.50 shipping charge

LOW BUDGET
WALL PHONES

Models:

Automatic Electric 50
and Kellogg 1100

These two model, reconditioned, wall-mounted units are ideal extension units where rugged and dependable telephones are needed, such as work areas, factories, garages, barns, warehouses and stores. They have an easy-access cradle. Complete for easy, trouble-free installation with dial, ringer, cable and plug. An outstanding value in two fine, distinctive models.

8-5011R—Black only $9.95
plus $1.50 shipping charge

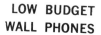

PLUG

Standard 4-prong telephone plug with color-indicated prongs for easy assembly.

8-283-B—Plug .... .99

WALL PANEL TELEPHONE

This handsome, flush-mounted panel telephone saves valuable space and is the latest development for a modern, built-in appearance in the home, office, school, or hotel. For most efficient installation it should be attached to wall studding during new construction when telephone service wiring costs less. This is a very attractive and trouble-free instrument. The 9¼ x 12½ panel is made of brushed aluminum, and it comes with 4 interchangeable colored vinyl inserts with adhesive backing for quick decorative color changes. Comes complete with handset and retractile cord, dial and ringer.

8-T95P $59.95
plus $1.50 shipping charge

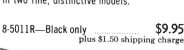

92

Radio Shack

Radio Shack is a 7-11 market type of operation; you pay a little extra for convenience. They have stores everywhere. They sell the usual hi-fi gear plus a lot of individual parts, hardware, and tools. I really hate to order parts by mail, especially for things I'm working on. Radio Shack makes it possible to just walk a few blocks and buy the transistor or whatever, right off a wall rack. In many cases I'll buy something from Radio Shack even though Poly-Paks has it cheaper. If you've never been in a Radio Shack Store, I'd recommend that you drop by just to look around. Often, I'll get an idea for a project just from seeing a component I hadn't known existed.

Compact AM/FM Stereo Radio System

89⁹⁵

With Built-In Quatravox®

- *Just Add Two Extra Speakers For 4-Channel Effects From Stereo Sources!*

Realistic Modulette™. Add vibrant stereo to any room! Sensitive tuner provides strong, clear reception. Features input for changer or tape player, stereo headphone jack, pushbutton power on/off, separate volume, balance and tone controls, stereo FM indicator, built-in antennas, inputs for external FM antenna. Walnut grained vinyl veneer cabinetry. 4¾x15⅝x10½". Each speaker, 10x8¼x5". With 13' speaker cables. U. L. listed. **12-1401** 89.95

Cassette Player/FM Stereo Radio

- *Sliding Volume, Balance And Tone Controls!*
- *Pushbutton Fast Forward, Rewind and Cassette Eject!*
- *Powerful Stereo Amplifier!*

Reg. ~~109⁹⁵~~

89⁹⁵

Be "in control" all the way with this 2-in-1 mobile music bargain! Play a cassette or listen to FM stereo with the realism you'd expect from a home stereo system. Insert cassette sideways and player starts instantly. Has end-of-tape indicator light. Radio has FM stereo light, mono/stereo switch, lighted dial. 2⅜x7½x8". With all hardware, power and speaker cables for under-dash mounting. 12 V neg. gnd. **12-1815** ....Sale 89.95

BIBLIOGRAPHY

Popular Mechanics DO-IT-YOURSELF ENCYCLOPEDIA
J.J. Little & Ives C.   New York.   1955

This is a 12-volume set of reprints from **Popular Mechanics Magazine**. It tells how to build just about anything you can think of; and some you wouldn't want to think of. It's great. Look for a set in thrift stores and at rummage sales.

Reader's Digest COMPLETE DO-IT-YOURSELF MANUAL
Reader's Digest. Pleasantville, New York.   1973. $12.99

I wouldn't wrap fish in **Reader's Digest**, but they've published a dynamite how-to book. For this I can almost forgive them their conning me into buying a subscription once with their lousy lottery ripoff.

The Sensuous Gadgeteer
Bill Abler.   Running Press, Philadelphia.   1973. $3.95

No kidding, this is a terrific book. Even if Running Press wasn't the publisher, I'd recommend it. Anyone can tell you how to use a tool; Bill Abler tells you how to use your head.

Underground Interiors: Adventures in Decorating and Design
Norma Skurka & Oberto Gili $5.95

This is a great idea book. It has color photos of some of the most amazing interior designs I've ever seen. Avant-garde would be a better adjective than underground, though. There isn't a crash pad in the lot.

Production Notes

Type, I.T.C. Souvenir
Composition by Alpha Publications, Inc.
Color separation & printing by Harrison Color Process Lithographers
Text Stock, Kimberly-Clark Lithofect Suede, 80 lb.
Cover Stock, Carolina Coated, 10 pt.